$5-
37.50
36-
#6545

GENERAL WILLIAM KING

Bath July 2d. 1821.

Dear Sir,
This will be handed you by Capt Curtis who proceeds to your place for one hundred casks of lime which have the goodness to furnish him and place to the amount of your Humble Servant.

William King

Ballard Green Esqr

GENERAL WILLIAM KING

Merchant, Shipbuilder, and Maine's First Governor

Marion Jaques Smith

Down East Books / Camden, Maine

Copyright 1980 Marion Jacques Smith
Library of Congress Catalog Card No. 79-67417
ISBN 0-89272-072-7

Designed by Ingrid Beckman
Printed at Twin City Printery / Lewiston, Maine

ACKNOWLEDGMENTS

IN this story of William King's life and the turbulent times in which he lived, emphasis has been placed on his business, ships, shipbuilding, and real estate, which led him into the military and political defense of the District of Maine and finally to governorship of the state.

Research into the vessels of William King, suggested by Dr. Charles Burden of the Bath Marine Museum, broadened as I learned more about King's life. The story of his vessels became in itself a short biography of the man who owned them. As such I hope it will be of interest to people from out of state as well as to those in Maine, and especially to citizens of Bath, where King lived for over fifty years, gained a fortune, and lost it.

My thanks go to Ann Hammond, Ralph Snow, Harold Brown, Nathan Lipfert, Doris Rowland, and Nancy Brown Gross of the Bath Marine Museum, who read, commented on and helped me with the research; also to Dr. Ronald Banks and Jane Stevens, who gave me information and encouragement.

Special thanks go to Thea Wheelwright, editor, and to my sister, Almena A. Thurston, who assisted me in the valuable research of William King's letters in the Maine Historical Society's archives in Portland. My thanks go also to the staff who assisted us, plus a patient and understanding husband who lent his support throughout.

MARION JAQUES SMITH

*This book is dedicated to
The Bath Marine Museum
where I began my
research into the life of
William King*

GENERAL WILLIAM KING

I

WILLIAM KING'S life story really begins with events that brought his father, Richard King, into the District of Maine to make a fortune and raise a family that was to take a leading part in the making of a nation and a state.

Richard settled in Watertown near Cambridge, Massachusetts, in 1740 at the age of twenty-two. There he kept a shop and was connected in business with Ebenezer Thornton, who was engaged in getting out timber for shipbuilding. Four years later, events in Europe interfered with Richard's business, for the colonists were again drawn into war.

In the spring of 1744, when Maria Theresa became heir to the Austrian throne, France joined Prussia in a war to gain territory in Austria. The English King, George III, as Elector of Hanover, made an alliance with Austria against France to protect the Queen. This was called King George's War in America and was the beginning of another struggle between the French and English for the control of its land and colonies.

Soon the French and their Indian allies attacked the English settlers in Nova Scotia, and French privateers were sent to prey upon New England's shipping. Governor Shirley of Massachusetts and merchants like Richard King, whose shipping business was threatened by privateers, decided to put a stop to this harassment.

Shirley appointed William Pepperell, a wealthy merchant of Kittery, to command the colonial forces; and sent out a squadron to join an English expedition against the strong fort at Louisburg on Cape Breton. Among his other appointments in 1745, Shirley made Richard King commissary of troops destined for Annapolis Royal, an important fort in Nova Scotia. It is possible that Pepperell had some influence in this appointment, for he and King were friends in the same business.

Much to everyone's astonishment, Pepperell succeeded in taking the French fort at Louisburg, and the harassment of shipping was ended, for which he was knighted by George III. Richard King had his reward, too. As soon as his service was over in 1746, he was able, with the profits he made as commissary at Annapolis, to pay off his mortgage on the Watertown property and dispose of it before moving to Dunstan's Landing in Scarborough in the District of Maine. There he not only dealt in lumber but bought three thousand acres of land, which was divided into several valuable farms. He had knowledge of legal forms and wrote with a good hand, so his services were in demand as a justice and conveyor of property as well as a trader.

Richard built a home midway between Portland (old Falmouth) and Saco, across from the great marsh in Scarborough. It was conveniently located on a creek that led out to sea and accommodated sailing craft of six to eight feet draught. His house began as a modest one-story cottage, to which he added a square two-story building as his family and fortune grew.

Richard's first wife was Isabella Bragdon, daughter of Samuel and Tabitha (Banks) Bragdon of York, Maine. They were married on November 20, 1753, and had three children, Rufus, Mary, and Paulina. Isabella died on October 19, 1759, soon after Paulina was born. On January 31, 1762, Richard married a cousin of his first wife, Mary Black, daughter of Samuel and Isabella (Bragdon) Black of York, Maine. The Bragdons were a family of worth and education and related by marriage to the Longfellow family of Portland.

The talent in Richard's family came from the father, according to William H. Smith, biographer of the King family. In those days not so much was said of the women, but Mary's influence should not be discounted.

William, born February 9, 1768, was the fourth child of this second marriage. He had an older brother, Richard Jr.; two older sisters: Isabella, who died at the age of six, and Dorcas; a younger sister Elizabeth (Betsy); and a brother Cyrus. Richard dearly loved his children, and he and Mary had a happy family life. For the oldest children he was able to afford the best education obtainable at that time. Rufus was sent to Dummer Academy in Byfield, Massachusetts, and on to Harvard College. Mary and Dorcas were taught at home by Richard himself, or by tutors, for Richard had a fair-sized library of his own. There were no schools in Scarborough at that time, a matter over which he was much concerned.

Richard prospered during the years preceding the Revolution. He became a wealthy merchant and owner of trading vessels and during hard times, when drought and great forest fires swept through the town, he became the creditor of a number of townsmen. At the time of the Stamp Riots in Boston, when feelings were high against public officials (or the British king's men), King was accused of being a Tory and was a victim of mob violence. Men with blackened faces, led by those who owed King money and envied him his position in the town and church affairs and termed themselves "Suns of liburty," smashed their way into his home and destroyed the interior. They paid special attention to his desk, seizing his financial records and other papers. None of his family records were left, and genealogists have no proof concerning to which branch of the King family Richard belonged. To date nothing in William's papers has been found that indicates who his father's parents were. Mary's family, however, may be traced through the Bragdon, Black, and Banks families.

At the beginning of the Revolution, Richard feared that a break with Great Britain would bring the Catholic French of Canada down upon Maine settlements, and he did not favor war. In 1774 it was learned that one of King's shipmasters had sold a cargo of lumber to the British in Boston. Although Richard was sick and ailing at the time, some militiamen forced him to mount a table and declare himself in favor of the Patriot cause. Loss of his business, the harassment by his enemies, and the humiliation he suffered may have contributed to his death, on March 27, 1775, at the age of fifty-seven.

Richard King left a valuable heritage to his country in his sons, who were to take a leading part in the formation of the State of Maine and our nation.

Mary King was left with six children to bring up: Paulina was sixteen; Richard Jr., thirteen; Dorcas, nine; William, seven and old enough to remember his father; Betsy, five; and Cyrus, four. Rufus was finishing his studies at Harvard, and Mary, the oldest daughter, had married Dr. Robert Southgate.

There is little to record about the family during the war years. Rufus completed his studies at Harvard and during the next year enlisted in the Continental Army, where he was assigned to General John Sullivan as aide-de-camp in Rhode Island.

Mary, like other mothers left to take care of their children during the war, had to live on the products of the farm. Aided by some of the servants, the boys tended farm chores and cared for the animals and gardens. Mary, assisted by her girls, assumed looking after the house and what business her husband had left. No doubt her son-in-law Dr. Southgate, who lived nearby, came to her assistance when needed.

Mary also took over her husband's task of educating the younger children and she is credited with teaching William his elementary subjects. She also made sure of their religious education and church affiliation, for it is recorded in the records of the First Congregational Church in Scarborough that on April 28, 1775, Elizabeth, William, and Cyrus, children of Richard and Mary King, were baptized.

When William was thirteen, he was sent to Phillips Academy in Andover, Massachusetts, for a term. It was said that the family thought he was meant for a mercantile life and that further learning and culture were not needed for that pursuit. This was to prove a handicap later when he entered political life, for his opponents laughed at his poor grammar and spelling, but this did not deter William from doing what he set out to do: to become a wealthy merchant and shipowner, as well as an outstanding politician.

Soon after William finished school, he went to work in a sawmill in Saco. It is thought that he worked in various other places but returned to Scarborough, where he kept his residence, and no doubt helped Richard Jr. on the farm. There are few records of his activities during these years, though it may be safe to say that he was learning the trades that had brought prosperity to his father.

During the time William was preparing himself for his future, the King family broke up. The girls were leaving for homes of their own: Paulina married Dr. Aaron Porter and was the first to leave; in 1786 Dorcas married Joseph Leland; Rufus had not returned home but had entered law practice in Newburyport in the office of Theophilus Parsons. In 1786 Rufus married Mary Alsop, daughter of John Alsop, a wealthy merchant of New York. He was selected as delegate to the Constitutional Convention of May 25, 1787. Highly successful, he was elected to the General Court in 1790 and chosen delegate to represent Massachusetts in the Continental Congress. Later, he moved to New York and was elected by its assembly as United States senator. He resigned after seven years in the Senate to become United States ambassador to England.

Betsy married Dr. Benjamin Jones Porter soon after Dorcas left home in 1786. Richard Jr. married Hannah Larrabee in 1790 and stayed in Scarborough. He was interested in building small sailing craft and in farming at Dunstan's Landing.

It seems reasonable to think that at about this time William felt free to set out for himself. He had gained a fair knowledge of sawmills and the lumber business and was confident that he could make his fortune in lumber, as his father had done.

Mary stayed on in the old home when William made his decision to leave. It must have been with pride that she said goodbye to this ambitious and forceful son. The home would be quiet, perhaps lonesome for a while, but she could look forward to correspondence and visits from children and grandchildren in the future, for she had a loving and caring family. William's letters show his close relationship with his brothers and sisters and their husbands and children. They were proud of their brother, coming to him for help and advice. In turn they worked for him, helping him in his business, with his family, and in political transactions when they could.

There is little doubt that Mary, as the years went by, took pride in the part her boys and girls played in their nation's affairs. Her nationalism was reflected even on her parlor walls. An observer wrote:

> We visited in the summer of 1884 what remains of the King mansion in Scarborough.... We were shown the inside of the old mansion not long before it was demolished, and remember as we

entered the best room our impressions of its mural paintings. One wall from the dado to the ceiling, was devoted to a painting called "Solomon's Temple;" another side of the room displayed what was called a representation of "The Enterprise and Boxer;" another showed an "Equestrian View of General Washington;" and over the mantel was emblazoned the "Arms of the United States," occupying the whole wall.

I think the artist's name was Osborn.[1]

II

THERE is a traditional story that William King left home to seek his fortune at the age of nineteen, with no definite place to go in mind, thinly clad, and driving a yoke of oxen, his only share in his father's estate. The census of 1790, however, lists him as living in Scarborough with Mary and Richard Jr. William had inherited land in Scarborough, which was unproductive then, but he had been working in various mills, was naturally frugal, and must have saved some money by this time. With his family background he was probably better clad than legend has it.

Betsy and her husband, Dr. Benjamin Porter, had moved to Topsham. William had been corresponding with his brother-in-law and no doubt had learned of the possibility of work in the sawmills and the vast untapped forestland "down east" where there were excellent prospects for a lumber business. He may have visited Bath, but more likely drove his oxen to Topsham in 1791 or 1792, where, on his brother-in-law's invitation, he came to live with the Porters, and went to work in a mill.

He was industrious, saved his money, and soon bought shares in the mill. On September 27, 1792, in company with Dr. Porter, he bought an acre and five rods of land in Topsham, paying twelve pounds, seventeen shillings and nine pence for his share. He and Porter formed a partnership under the name of Porter & King —

Merchants and opened a store in Topsham on the southwest corner of Winter and Main streets. Porter assumed control of the store and King devoted himself chiefly to the lumber business. Later that year, Porter had a fine mansion built at 26 Elm Street in Topsham.* It was an unusually large colonial home for that time, set back from the road, with a traditional hip roof and chimneys. It had Goergian-style sidelights and a fanlight over the door, which added to the grace of the house. King stayed here with the Porters until he moved to Bath in late 1799 or 1800.

Stories and letters kept by his associates and family add to our knowledge of King's character and business. They said he was impatient over small details and preferred to pursue the broader aims of the business, leaving other matters to his partner. A traditional story, told many years after, points to this attitude:

> Happening to be in the store one day with the business of which he was not very familiar, a woman came in to buy some needles. The general handed her some, and she asked the price. "Ah!" said he, "I suppose about a cent apiece." The thrifty housewife rejoined that she could buy enough elsewhere at the rate of three or four for a cent. "Ah!" said he, "if that is the case, take the whole; throw them out; I will have nothing in my store that is not worth a cent!"[1]

A letter written on July 16, 1793, to his youngest brother, Cyrus, at Andover Academy, shows William's affection for him and also gives a clue to his own financial standing that year. He offered, if Cyrus did not qualify to proceed as he planned at graduation — and was agreeable — to make him his partner in business and share equally in the profits from his land, shipping, and mills.

Cyrus appreciated his brother's generous offer, for he kept the letter carefully among his papers. But he did qualify to become a lawyer and like their brother Rufus became a brilliant one. William did not think any the less of his brother for not taking advantage of his offer; he was proud of Rufus's success and kept up his interest in him and in his family after Cyrus's death.

William felt close to his brothers and sisters and their children,

---

*Occupied by Captain Elmer Hill in 1978.

helping the boys when he could with their financial problems and some of the girls with their education. In 1800, while in Boston, he took time from his business to entertain his sister Mary's daughter, Eliza Southgate, who was visiting there. Eliza stated in a letter to her sister Octavia in Scarborough, "Uncle William King has been very attentive to me — carried me to the play 3 or 4 times and to all the balls and assemblies excepting the last which I went with Mr. Andrews."[2]

Between 1792 and 1799, Porter and King increased their business by buying a fourth share in Brigadier Thompson's "Great Mill" for $666.66. They expected to own all but a fourth of the mill by 1804. King also bought a farm in Topsham with a good growth of timber on it. About this time lumber from their mill that cost about $8.00 per thousand feet could be sold in the West Indies for $60 to $100 per thousand. Prospects were good for business, but they needed transportation for their products.

In 1792 merchants had to provide their own means of transportation, so in addition to setting up their store and operating a lumber mill, in order to carry their own and associates' products to market, Porter & King began shipbuilding in Topsham and Brunswick. They had the lumber, and other equipment could be obtained in Boston.

Their first shipyards were probably temporary ones built on the shores of the Androscoggin River close to the mill. Shipyards had few if any buildings in those days. Shipwrights and carpenters, due to the sporadic nature of the shipbuilding business, were often farmers and fishermen who worked in the shipyards whenever there was work. Yards of this period rarely employed more than ten men, and often less, for the construction of a single vessel.

On the sloping river bank they erected building ways of logs, hewn flat on one side and set in the ground parallel to the water's edge. The ways extended far out into the river so that the vessel was supported until it was in water deep enough to float it when it was launched bow-first. Since vessels were constructed in the open at this time, on stormy days the workers might have stayed home or gone to the mill to whittle treenails (pronounced *trunnels*) of locust or oak, or to work on some other small job they could do under cover.

King, owner of the mill and familiar with the timber needed, could furnish hackmatack, white oak, beech, elm, birch, spruce, and all the various hard and soft woods needed from his land or from farmers near by. White pine for masts, however, was already getting scarce locally and probably had to be brought from upcountry. King was close enough to the shipyards to oversee the shaping of their vessels under construction by the masterbuilder and carpenters as they worked with whipsaws, broadaxes, adzes, pod augers, and the new-fangled spiral augers.

Porter & King had five vessels built in Topsham and Brunswick with which to begin their trading, consisting of one brig, two ships, and two schooners. Their first vessels, the brig *Nancy* and the schooner *Minerva,* were built in Brunswick in 1793, and the schooner *Guardian* in 1795. The ships *Adrastus* and *Osiris* were built in Topsham in 1794 and 1796. They had billetheads and square sterns and were adapted to carry the cargoes that the partners planned to send along the Atlantic coast to the West Indies, South America, and Europe. Robert Lapish, local businessman, had shares in the *Adrastus* and some of their other vessels. Sylvanus Cushing, also local, shared in the costs of the *Guardian.*

Porter & King also bought the *Rebecca,* built in Freeport in 1795. It is thought that King bought or had shares in the *Eagle,* a vessel that sailed out of Boston, before he went into business with Porter, but there is some doubt of his ownership by 1799, for he was anxious to have his part of the cargo in her discharged in order to save expenses of chartering.

The partners had no trouble in finding cargoes to add to their lumber for the West Indies trade. Shipyards were in need of masts, spars, and hewn timber. Products of the cooper's trade were in demand, such as shooks or staves, hoops and heads for casks, hogsheads, tierces and barrels of various kinds. These were packed in bundles and assembled when they reached their destination. Consigners filled them with molasses, sugar, and rum and they came back bringing more profit on the homeward voyage. Some vessels carried on top of their lumber flat-bottomed craft known as "Moses boats," which some planters bought to carry their molasses out on the narrow streams bordering their plantations to vessels anchored in deeper waters offshore. At times King's vessels also carried prefabricated houses to the West Indies.

King found that, in addition to lumber, farm products were in demand. Cattle and horses were needed on the plantations, as well as food products such as onions, parsnips, potatoes, grain, flour, meat and fish, either pickled or salted. To these he added apples from his farm, a product his father had sold before him.

Although the name District of Maine had been legally conferred on the Province of Maine by an Act of Congress in 1778, the partners often received mail addressed to "the Province of Maine" or "Bath on the Kennebec." Duplicate or triplicate copies of important papers or letters were sent for fear some might be lost. Copies were also given to captains in port at the same time, and the captains would deliver or mail them when they arrived in the United States.

Though the partners gave their captains and agents in various ports letters of instruction for disposal of their cargoes, there was such competition for business with other traders, that it was often left to the captains to bargain or to barter the goods for what they could get.*

In some ways business conditions were good in 1792. President Washington had kept the new and weak United States neutral in the war between Great Britain and France. Alexander Hamilton, Secretary of Treasury, had placed money affairs on a sound basis, opening the way for trade with Europe. Both England and France did not wish to use their ships in trade and were in need of supplies.

In other ways, it was an unsettled and troubled world into which Porter & King were so confidently launching their business. In Europe the French people, for years oppressed by the greedy court policies of their rulers, had turned on them in 1789 and eventually beheaded King Louis XVI, his Queen, and several thousand of France's ruling class in a bloody revolution. Flushed with their success, the French Assembly had declared war on Europe's monarchies. Holland, Austria, and Prussia had joined Great Britain in a coalition to protect themselves, but had finally dropped out of the conflict, one by one, leaving Great Britain to fight France alone.

By 1794 King had become a man of importance in Topsham and

---

* A message King received from the captain of the *Nancy*, at Demarara, British Guiana, August 10, 1810, reads: "I arrived here after a passage of 47 days, sold my cows for $72 and took my pay in rum and molasses. Sixty head of cows arrived before me and sold for $64 each."

Brunswick. He was one of the incorporators of the Topsham-Brunswick toll bridge over the Androscoggin River. It was not only a considerable help to the towns but it helped his business, too.

A description of him by John H. Sheppard shows how he impressed those around him. ". . . In his person, he was tall and of a striking figure, and with a finely formed head, strongly marked features, high forehead, and black impending brows, he had a natural and majestic air of command, which impressed every beholder with respect. . . . He had his faults, but he had many admirers."[3] A painting done by Gilbert Stuart in repayment of a loan shows him as a handsome young man at this age. Stuart did one of King's wife Ann at the same time.[*] The portraits now hang in the Law Library at the State House in Augusta.

It is not surprising that with such an appearance and personality King was elected to represent Topsham at General Court in Boston in 1795 and 1796. In 1800, when he decided to move to Bath on the Kennebec, he continued his political career as a senator from Lincoln County in the District of Maine. In the legislature he soon became a leader and as Deane Dudley, of Kingfield, who as a boy remembered King well, remarked, "His look was a personification of dignity. So conspicuous was he in every circle where he moved, that the most indifferent observer failed not to notice him."[4] This leadership was to help him in improving conditions for the people of the District of Maine.

If William had ever gone barefoot as a young man, he had surely earned his shoes by now. It was said of King after he moved to Bath, that he and Peleg Tallman were the only two men who possessed boots decent enough to represent the town in Boston. This was probably not true, but it does establish them as well-dressed men of the town, outstanding among their fellow townsmen.

King's election as representative and senator in Boston served him a double purpose, for he could not only serve his town and county in the legislature, but his own business in that city. While there he found time to contact and become acquainted with shipping agents, business firms and banks, and to learn how he could extend his

---

[*] The paintings were sent to Bath by Frazier, Savage & Co., of Boston, in April 1806, on the brig *Calista*.

business. His letters reveal that Porter & King had become known in many ports where agents contacted him for business.

It was in 1794, while the partners were getting their vessels ready for trade, that news came of John Jay's treaty with Great Britain. Though not everyone was happy with its provisions, it opened trade with the British East Indies and, when the treaty was ratified, with the West Indies. It was no longer necessary to smuggle in goods to the colonists there who preferred American merchandise to British, as many had done. The Spanish, learning of the treaty with Great Britain that same year, decided to deal with the United States under the Pinckney Treaty, which gave the Americans the right to use the Mississippi River and docks at New Orleans. Americans along the river could now ship their products by sea to coastal cities, the Indies, and Europe. This was good reason for the partners to enlarge their cargo-carrying business, and King began studying how he could take advantage of it.

He soon found out that it would not be all clear sailing to the West Indies. Spain was allied with France against Great Britain in 1797. French and Spanish privateers were prowling the Carribean. The French were angry with the United States over provisions in Jay's Treaty that did not protect them from British war vessels. Harassment of American traders followed. French cruisers even came as far north as Maine. Captain Hatch reported escaping one in the fog off Seguin at the mouth of the Kennebec.

The French revolutionists had made France a republic, but they had been ruled so long by a king that they had not learned how to govern themselves; in spite of this, they had been successful in war. Good soldiers were promoted rapidly under war conditions. One of these men, Napoleon Bonaparte, had risen to be general of the armies of France. He used his power to seize the weak new government and make himself dictator of France in 1799. This change in government was to affect Porter & King's trade in the West Indies, the Southern states, and European countries, for Napoleon took over the islands and Louisiana and attempted to destroy Great Britain's trade.

Because the United States was neutral it would seem that Porter & King would be free to do business with any nation, but it did not take them long to learn that a neutral nation, especially a new weak one like the United States, would often be treated with contempt. However, they determined to go ahead, believing the profits would more than make up for any losses they might have.

They were fortunate at first, for they had no trouble with privateers until April 1, 1799, and it was a Spanish privateer that caused it, proving that being neutral was no protection. Their brig, the *Nymph,* under Captain Raymond, sailed for Ciudad Trujillo (Dominican Republic today) with a load of boards. She had been chartered by some merchants in New York to carry lumber to St. Domingo. On the way Captain Raymond found it necessary to go to Havana for water. In the Carribean the *Nymph* was attacked and captured by a privateer, plundered, and stripped of her cargo.

Captain Raymond was held prisoner in Cuba for a long time. As soon as he was free, he began a suit for the release of the *Nymph* and reimbursement of her cargo. When he found the Cuban tribunal had no intention of restoring his vessel or paying for her cargo, he appealed to the Spanish admiralty in Madrid, with no results. He wrote to King that Spanish justice was no better than Cuban. The *Nymph* rotted at her moorings in Cuba, never to return to her home port.

It wasn't until November 28, 1799, that Porter & King had trouble again, this time with the French. Captain Tristam Redman in the ship *Osiris,* after unloading her cargo at Liverpool, England, set out for New York with a return cargo of twelve ton 600 weight of coal, loose; 175 tons of white salt, 64 crates of earthenware, and other merchandise on November 23, 1799. There were nine seamen and three passengers on board with the captain. On December 5, 1799, at latitude 5:30 degrees north and longitude 9:30 degrees west, the ship was captured by a French corsair, the *Bouganville,* carrying 24 guns and a 100-man crew. Captain Redman was taken with his papers aboard her for four hours, while the French crew plundered the *Osiris*'s cargo, taking what they wanted. The French then took the three passengers aboard the corsair and returned the captain and a prize crew of a lieutenant and seven French crewmen to take charge of the *Osiris.*

The prize crew set out with the ship for a French port. The Americans, now prisoners in their own vessel, began to plot to recapture her. On January 4, 1800, they took the French crew by surprise. While the sailors were aloft reefing sails, Captain Redman secured the French lieutenant, and the mate took the man at the wheel. The American seamen stood by with handspikes and captured the Frenchmen as they came down from aloft, thus giving the Maine men full charge of their ship again. They were near the English Channel and encountering heavy weather, went into the Lough of Belfast, steered for St. Georges Channel, and arrived at Yarmouth the evening of January 7. They landed and turned the Frenchmen over to the commander of His Majesty's garrison at Belfast. Here also, according to the law, Captain Redman made his protest on the condition of the ship.

The *Osiris* had been insured for $6,000 in 1799. The report of the Marine Insurance Co. in Boston to the vessel's owners detailed the complete salvage, sales, and repair of the *Osiris,* and Porter & King's loss was $31,997.50.

III

WILLIAM King had seen and appreciated the advantage of the long reach at Bath as an excellent place for shipbuilding and trading, requiring much less navigation to reach the ocean than Topsham. Isaiah Crooker, John Clarke, Peleg Tallman, Dummer Sewall, and others were already in business there, and at the south end of the reach Jonathan Davis had a store, wharf, and shipbuilding business. His decision made, King bought land from Joshua Shaw, a speculator in land on the "Point." Henry Owen in an article in the *Bath Daily Times*, of July 6, 1920, explains the term "Point":

> Sometimes, even today, one hears someone, usually an oldtimer, refer to the business district of Bath as the "Point." Since the waterfront in that locality follows practically a straight line, geographical appearances do not seem to warrant that expression, but when Bath was being settled, the elevation crowned now by the Davenport Memorial City Hall was actually a bluff, connected with the mainland only by a narrow isthmus and almost surrounded by tidewater. This peninsula got to be called Shaw's Point because of speculative purchase of the larger part of it by Joshua Shaw in 1792. Just before and after 1800 the "Point" was beginning to be built up. Vine St. provided the earliest access and marked the neck connecting the "Point" with the mainland.

King began shipbuilding in Bath in 1797 and 1798 with the brig

GENERAL WILLIAM KING 17

Ferdinand. We do not have a description of his shipyard, but know that it was located about where the Central Maine railroad tracks cross the Carleton Bridge today. It was probably better equipped than his earlier temporary yards, and it had a slipway cut down into the river bank, the sides being shored up with logs and pilings. The typical yard of that time had a long shed open on one side, where the men worked in bad weather. On the floor above in the shed was a mold loft where the vessel's plans were laid out full-size, and patterns for her timber were made. A small joiner's shop, a blacksmith's shop, and a storage shed were other usual buildings. The yard would also have had a sawpit, for it was doubtful that the Topsham mill would have been able to cater to all their needs. King's office was probably in his store, built sometime during the summer of 1799 next to the shipyard.

In 1799 vessels were built mostly of local woods. King is credited with being one of the first to use southern yellow pine for planking and ceiling the hull of his vessels, indicating that he was content not only to use the best materials at hand but the hard pine from the south that had been found to be more durable. This did not become a practice, however, until the 1830s. Timbers for vessels were selected on expeditions to the woods and often arrived at the shipyard, squared, shaped, and numbered. Upon their arrival, the keel was stretched or laid, balanced on keel blocks that were arranged to give it an incline of about ⅝ of an inch to the foot, sloping to the water. The stem and stern posts and all their supporting pieces were set into place. The vessel was framed, planked, and the ceiling put in, the decks installed, and the finish done in the cabins. Hull and decks were caulked and finally the vessel was rigged. This last process might take place before or after the vessel was in the water, although it was always started before the launch. Thus King's vessels were built in Bath. Occasionally a vessel was loaded and provisioned when it was launched.

Planking, caulking, rigging, and other specialized jobs in later years were frequently done by independent crews who traveled from yard to yard, working wherever their skills were needed.*

---

* King's vessels were often larger than the average. Some, including the *Perserverance,* the *Ann,* the *Confidence,* the *Reserve* and the *Resolution* were among the largest vessels built locally.

When King settled in Bath, Peter H. Green became his partner in the Bath store, while Porter continued to operate the Topsham business.

Green is listed as building for himself the brigs *Huron*, 246 tons, and *Radius*, 156 tons, in 1815. He built the brig *Transit*, 199 tons, in 1818.

It was not long before King became a powerful figure in Bath. Henry Owen writes, in his *History of Bath, Maine:*

> We have referred to the last third of the 18th Century as the age of Dummer Sewall. In like manner, the first 30 years or so of the 19th Century were the age of William King, who was the dominant figure in local affairs during that epoch. As the century began quite a number of able and enterprising men had settled in Bath, but of them all, King was without doubt the ablest and most enterprising. His activities embraced every field — politics, government, commerce and trade, shipbuilding, farming, real estate, religion and military affairs — and in whatever group or undertaking he found himself, he was the dominant figure. He was not a cultured man, in the usual sense of the word; but he was a man of good judgment, strong character, and indomitable pluck, for years generally successful in his business ventures as well as his other undertakings, and apparently no undertaking was too great for him to tackle with utmost intrepidity. He was about 30 years old when he came to Bath, and was already a man of means and position, though he began life with nothing but his native ability.[1]

While King was serving as a representative from Topsham in Boston he became associated in business with John Frazier of Frazier & Savage, charter merchants in Boston. He visited the Frazier home where John lived with his mother and young sister.

Mixing pleasure with business the winter season of 1799 and 1800, William invited his niece Eliza Southgate, who was visiting in Boston, to plays, assemblies and balls. Eliza was a lively and likable girl and did not lack for partners at the balls, so her Uncle William was often left to find other partners. Here he met, and probably did not neglect to dance with, his business associate's pretty young sister, Ann N. Frazier. No doubt he found her a delightful dancer and sought her out as often as he could. At the end of the season Eliza asked her uncle if he minded if she went to the last assembly with a Mr. Andrews. William was far from hurt by her request and asked Ann to attend the assembly with him. Eliza, tired with the busy social life in Boston, returned to Saco, while William, when in Boston, became a frequent visitor in the Frazier home. He had fallen in love with lovely eighteen-year-old Ann. She was graceful and shy with retiring manners, quite the opposite of the dominant King, and it was no wonder she fell in love with this handsome, successful young businessman. She was the youngest daughter of Elizabeth and Captain Phoenix Frazier. Her father had died when she was very young, and she was left in her mother's care. In addition to her brother John, her older sister's husband, E. L. Boyd, had business dealings with King in Boston.

There is no account of the quiet wedding that took place or of their trip to Bath, but when William introduced his bride to society in the church in the Erudition building, it was said that Mrs. King was "welcomed into Bath's best society, became a leader, and all through her life universal deference was accorded her many lovely traits of character."[2]

By the time William and his wife arrived in Bath his shipyard was in operation and his home was being built above it on a bluff at the Point. An article in the Bath *Daily Times* of January 1, 1912, gives the approximate date of the building of this house. A carpenter remodeling the old Governor King's home, it states, discovered in a room on the second floor, plainly written under the mantel, the date June 17, 1798, signed Ebenezer Chase, one of the original workmen. It was reported that the structure was made of the finest lumber to be found at this time, for King was particular about the home into which he was bringing his bride. Some of the timbers were of white oak 12x14 inches. The parlor mantel piece was made of iron with mother of pearl inlay.

During the process of the building of their home, the Kings lived in the timber tavern kept by Major Edward Page on High Street, which was located not very far from the present County Courthouse. The King's house, in the beginning, was a story and a half structure, to which he added as he became more prosperous. It was built facing north, looking up the river. Parker Reed in his *History of Bath,* written in 1894, gives a picture of it as it was in King's prosperous years:

His mansion which he built in Bath stood, in the Governor's time, near the banks of the Kennebec, on the site of the present (now former) Custom House. The grounds were extensive; old-fashioned flowers and shrubs filled the front yard, while on the west and north was an extensive orchard of fine fruit trees, the pride of the Governor, and which was enclosed by a high stone wall. This house, in its palmy days, with its ample hall, broad stair-case, its chambers, with high post bedsteads and draperies, the coat-of-arms on the wall, the parlor, with its massive furniture, and French plate mirrors over the mantel, the silver service, with convex mirrors, the candles blazing in the winter twilight above the glowing fire on the broad hearth, all going to make a picture of beauty and comfort. He was a great entertainer. With unbounded hospitality his house was the resort, from time to time, of eminent men and women of this and foreign lands. There was not one who could outdo him in table argument, and though often forcible and abrupt in his speech to men, his manners were always gentle and courteous to ladies and children. His evenings were often devoted to whist, and it was even a common thing in those days to devote a portion of the day to cards, and General King's card parties came to be a decided feature in Bath society. There was the Governor in the showy costume of the day, ruffed, starched and frilled, seated in state in his long parlor, where his friends assembled. They would sit at cards until late in the evening, not forgetting a cup of tea for the ladies and a glass of wine for the gentlemen. There used to be hot rubbers (in which two out of three of the five games had to be played in order to break the series.) The gay dames of a quiet day, sitting around the parlor, and the fresh breeze blowing through the open windows, where one could sit and look up and down the Kennebec; then in the twilight his servant would harness up the span and drive the guests to their homes.[3]

With the religious training his mother had given him, it was natural that William would want to join the church in the town he had chosen to make his home. Dummer Sewall's account book notes that on July 15, 1800, William King contributed three dollars to the church, which gives a general idea of when he joined. At this time there was a disagreement between the orthodox and liberal Congregationalists over the choice of ministers. Their meetings had been in the meetinghouse below Witch Spring on the Berry's Mill road, now marked by the old cemetery. When King joined, most of the congregation had moved their meetings to the Erudition schoolhouse, located then at what is now the northeast corner of Center and High streets. This was nearer the growing center of town. The town officials appointed a committee of both factions to supply a minister who would be paid from town taxes. King was soon appointed to the committee to find a minister, along with Dummer Sewall, Joshua Shaw, Thomas Lemont, and Samuel Davis. Finally the orthodox group, unable to agree on doctrine, obtained the right to be exempt from the town tax and was allowed to raise money for their church group by taxing pews.

King, inclined to be liberal, was soon at odds with some members of the orthodox church group. In 1802, they built the North Church next to the Erudition school building and King had stormy sessions with some of the members. It was said that one churchman criticized King's card playing and remarked that it led to cheating and that he always used to cheat whenever he played. King's reply came quick as a flash, "Ah!, I dare say this is true, but you need have no fear for me; I never allow myself to play in such company as yours."[4]

King was never a drinking man, but there was always wine on his table. Reed writes: "On one occasion a judge was dining with him and refused wine on the plea that he was a member of a temperance society. Melons were brought in at dessert and the General poured wine on his; his guest did the same; a short time after a physician was dining with the General, he also refused wine, when King bluffly remarked, 'Won't you have a spoon Doctor? Recently Judge Blank was dining with me and he would not drink my wine but he ate it with a spoon'" King, it seems, had no sympathy for insincerity.

Finally, not being able to agree with the minister and people of the North Church, King joined a liberal group who were meeting in the old meetinghouse. This was not convenient, so King and his group purchased two lots on South Hill, overlooking the river on the east side of High Street near Union Street. They hired Tilson Cushing a mechanic and citizen of some importance in Bath, as masterbuilder. In July 1804 the South Church was completed.

King was entrusted to find a minister for the church when he went to Boston on business. He was much impressed with young Mr.

William Jenks and asked him to be their first minister. Jenks was a graduate of Harvard College and a Congregationalist, but the local clergymen declined to install him on the grounds that there was no church. "When this state of facts was made known at a meeting of the South Society, Mr. King promptly exclaimed, 'We must have a church, must we? I'll have one immediately.' He sat down and wrote a document to be signed by such as were willing to enroll themselves as members. To quiet any conscientious scruples any might have in belonging to a church when not a professor of religion, he explained that their wishing to organize a church was simply a form and matter of business. Signing the paper himself, he took it around for others to sign, and very soon obtained the required number. On returning home from the meeting, he explained to his wife what he had done, and asked her to head the list for lady members. She said, 'I cannot, I cannot.' 'Why not?' asked he. Said she, 'I am not good enough, you know I am not a Christian.' 'Ah,' said he, 'jine, Annie, jine, I have jined, and you are a d....d sight better Christian than I am.' She 'jined' and the church was founded."[6]

It was probably because of this experience with the church in Bath as well as other experiences with church people, that King, while serving in General Court in 1811, sponsored and helped pass the Toleration Act, which did away with the law that obliged towns to tax the people to support a minister. He felt people should be free to support their own church and belief.

In 1835 when the South Society, with some additions, emerged as the third Congregationalist Church Parish, William King's name was not on the membership list. Later, when hard times fell on the Old South Church and it was inactive, the Kings came to the Winter Street Church, built by the North Society on the north corner of Washington and Winter streets in 1843. Ann many have influenced him to return to the church where she felt more at home.

The South Church was sold by the new group, who built the Central Church in 1847 at the foot of Washington Street hill above Center Street. In 1854 the Old South Church was burned by a mob of Know Nothing Party members because it had been rented to Catholics. By this time William King was past caring about its fate.

IV

SINCE vessels were a vital part of his business as it grew, King continued building one or two a year in Bath and replaced those he lost or sold. Sometimes he chartered other vessels for cargoes when his own were in use and he took other associates to share expenses. He built up a network of contacts with commercial houses in Boston, New York, Philadelphia, Baltimore, Norfolk, Savannah, Petersburg, and other southern ports. His vessels went to the West Indies, Demerara, and the Dutch settlements in South America. In Europe he traded mostly with the ports of Liverpool and London in England, and Cork and Belfast in Ireland; from there his vessels sometimes went to France, Holland, and later Spain and Portugal, but the bulk of his trade was in England and Ireland. At times merchants there quoted their prices and the merchandise they needed and chartered his vessels for their own use.

Communication was slow in this business and much depended on sailing conditions. It took weeks and sometimes months for messages from captains and business houses to reach Porter & King's offices.

Most of King's captains and crews were from the District of Maine or Massachusetts. For example, on one voyage the men who shipped out on the brig *Androscoggin* were: master and first mate from Brunswick, one seaman from Lynn, Massachusetts, two from

Boothbay, one from Bath, and a black seaman from Philadelphia. Seamen were hired when needed and released when the vessels were idle for some time. Captains transferred from one ship to another, as King directed.

The partners were making money in 1799, but it was not all clear sailing. A storm hit the new brig *Ferdinand* off Newfoundland on the way back from England. Captain Bosworth made his protest in Newfoundland, making known the condition of the vessel before a notary, and wrote to Porter that she would have to have new masts, rigging, and sails before they could get to Boston, then to Bath for added repairs. This happened in May, and in June a squall hit the *Osiris* on her way back from the West Indies, with much the same results. Repairs were made, however, and the vessels put back into service to earn more than enough to pay expenses.

The Industrial Revolution was taking place in England, bringing weaving out of the home and into the factory. This greatly increased the demand for cotton. King, interested in this demand and alert to seize the opportunity to provide more cargoes for his vessels, called Captain Nehemiah Harding into his office in Bath and asked him to investigate the cotton trade in New Orleans. When the captain asked him where to find the port of New Orleans, King replied vaguely that it was somewhere in the Gulf of Mexico. He had learned of the treaty with Spain that opened trade to Amerians there, but he left the details of navigation up to the captain. Fortunately Captain Harding obtained an old Spanish chart and managed to find New Orleans to begin a cotton-carrying trade for Bath ships that was to last over eighty years. After an assurance of a supply of cotton, King became principal owner with Ezra Smith and Dr. Porter in the first cotton mill in Brunswick. They made cotton thread and yarn, but not much money for the firm.

Encouraged by their success, King had the *Reunion* built in Bath in 1800, and she paid her cost three times over when first put in service. On November 20, 1801, Porter wrote to King in Boston, congratulating him on the successful launch of his new ship (probably the *Volunteer*, which King had built for himself), and the safe arrival of the *Reunion* at Liverpool, but expressing great pessimism concerning the prospect of immediate peace between England and France. He predicted a great change in their carrying trade, for war conditions added to the risks they were already taking.

There was soon trouble with the English in the West Indies. One of King's agents, Mark Dyett, wrote to Porter & King from Montserrat on December 4, 1800, that the British man-o-war *Hornet* had just brought in their brig *Nancy* on suspicion of having infringed the revenue laws. Dyett had protested to the British Judge of Admiralty, who had freed the *Nancy* for only a small tax, which Dyett had paid. Dyett had also provided Captain Lane with provisions. In return for these favors, he asked Porter & King to send him cargoes to sell. He enclosed an order for boards, fish, staves, and a few boxes of spermaccti candles. Some months later Dyett wrote again, reminding them of the favor he had done them and asking them to send the order, but the partners were having difficulties sending cargoes to their destinations.

The month before, the brig *Alexander*, on her way to Jamaica, was captured by a French armed vessel and held six days until she was recaptured by the United States schooner *Enterprise*, William Shaw, commander, and ordered into St. Kitts, where the agent for the recapture had retained one half the price of the brig and cargo as salvage. King heard this through his friend Silas Lee, of Wiscasset, who informed him that the United States law allowed agents only one eighth of the cargo and release of the vessel to the owners. King, angry at the dishonesty of his own countrymen, protested to Washington to restore his cargo and vessel. His brig was returned, but there is nothing said in his letters about the return of his cargo. After this incident, it was a relief to receive a letter from their captain, John Saunders, in St. Kitts, saying he was sailing home in a fleet of twenty merchantmen under the protection of the United States ship *Maryland*, Captain Rogers, master. The merchant captains had to call on the United States Navy to insure their safety on the way home.

From 1801 to 1803 there was a brief period of peace. Both France and Great Britain sought relief in the Peace of Amiens. Napoleon wanted time to strengthen his government to continue his struggle for empire, and Great Britain was passing through the Industrial Revolution and was in debt. Under the terms of peace, France gained back most of her territory and Great Britain retained

Trinidad and Dutch possessions in Ceylon. Porter & King took advantage of the peace to increase their cotton and produce trade to Europe and the West Indies.

King put his new ship, the *Volunteer,* into the cotton-carrying trade under the command of Captain Bosworth, who probably had an interest in the cargo, according to the letter he wrote King, saying that he had filled the cabin so full that he could hardly creep in on his hands and knees. The ship was loaded so heavily that two of Bosworth's crew ran away and swore they would not go to sea in her, she was so deep.

King kept the *Volunteer* in trade until 1803. News that Napoleon was planning to cut off the cotton trade may have influenced him to sell the vessel in July of that year to his agent James Anderson and a Mr. Winthrop in Philadelphia.

King's fears for his cotton as well as his produce trade were not without reason. Encouraged by his gains, Napoleon planned to re-establish French authority in the West Indies and ordered Spain to turn Louisiana over to him and close the port of New Orleans to United States merchants. He prepared an expedition to Haiti and San Domingo, but it failed. Twenty officers and thirty thousand of his men died of fever in the island swamps. Although he had just acquired the territory of Louisiana, Napoleon decided to sell it to the United States. He was ready to go to war with Great Britain again and needed money; also he feared that he might lose the territory anyway to the British.

It was welcome news to Porter & King in December 1803 when the Stars and Stripes were raised over New Orleans. William prepared to resume his cotton trade. He had lost his ship *Confidence,* which had been wrecked at the entrance to the river at Bordeaux, France; and he was now encouraged to build another to take her place. The *United States* and the *Reserve,* the only vessel in his fleet with a figurehead, were built in 1804. Both vessels were needed, for while he was in Boston, William heard from Porter that the *Ferdinand* was in trouble again. Captain Lane had written from Trinidad (April 27, 1804) that he arrived there in twenty-eight days from Wilmington; that the day he sailed the brig had sprung a leak, which had obliged him to keep both pumps going the whole voyage and he was under the necessity of throwing off part of the deck load and selling the remainder of the cargo for $250, the market being very poor in Trinidad.

In December Porter wrote that he had sold the *Ferdinand* for $3,500, saying the report of her condition so affected the crew that he believed another crew could not be obtained and Captain Lane was so staggered by it that he offered fifty dollars to be released from going to sea in her again.

Interests allied to trading and shipping were also important to King. It is not surprising that in connection with his growing business, and knowing the risks to shipping in 1802, he had joined his associates and become a trustee of the Marine Insurance Co. of Boston. He could thus have some protection for his vessels, and shares in the company would bring in money.

In addition to the insurance business, he joined some of his friends in establishing a bank in Wiscasset in the District of Maine. The town was a thriving business center at that time. King was made president of the Lincoln and Kennebec Bank of Wiscasset and served in that capacity until he retired in 1807.* He had also become a corporate member of the Hallowell and Augusta Bank, a branch of the Wiscasset Bank.

In 1812 King became president of his own bank in Bath, for he realized that the growing shipbuilding business in his home town needed financial support. His Bath Bank was erected on the south corner of Front and Center streets, across from his home. Soon after King estalbished it, a rival bank was erected on the north corner of Front and Center streets by Jonathon Hyde and Peleg Tallman.

There was enough business for two banks, for the shipbuilding industry required capital and insurance. Bankers could handle the merchants' letters of credits, loan notes, and the drawing up of bills of lading. A list of stockholders in King's banks soon read like a who's who in shipbuilding circles of those days.

Banks issued their own paper money then. Frequently bills pictured vessels of different kinds, such as sloops, topsail schooners, brigs and ships.

Along with his growing shipping and banking business, William

---

* The stockholders, in appreciation for his services, at that time gave him a plate worth $500. He kept his shares and interest in the bank for some time after.

kept an interest in transportation between Bath and Brunswick. He had been a charter member in the first Cumberland turnpike and had some knowledge of how a turnpike was built and managed. In 1804 he felt there was need to improve transportation between the two towns. He obtained a charter for a turnpike, which he built and chiefly managed. It began at the north side of what is now the courthouse lot and ran directly to the New Meadows River, which it crossed by a bridge midway between the location of the old Bull Rock Bridge and today's Railroad Bridge. It shortened the distance to Brunswick, being more direct than the old road, which skirted the upper end of the New Meadows marsh.

Money earned in trade and shipping did not all go back into shipping. King invested in real estate, particularly farm and timberlands, as the early records show. He liked to raise crops for trade, such as apples and potatoes for his cargoes. In 1807, while serving in the Massachusetts Legislature, William and several of his political associates, including Harrison Gray Otis, obtained title to three townships in the Bingham Purchase in Franklin County. Peleg Tallman was also interested in this land, which included what is now Kingfield, Concord, and Lexington townships, but while he was in Bath arranging to finance it, King and his associates made arrangements with the Bingham heirs to take it over. Tallman never quite forgave King for this sharp deal and William lived to regret it.

King bought his associates' claims in 1809 and took over the management of his "Million Acre Farm," as it was called. It was his dream to establish a thriving and profitable lumbering and farming community there. His wife Ann is credited with naming it Kingfield for him on one of their visits to the farm.

Because he was concerned for settlers who improved the unsettled land, it was chiefly due to King's efforts in the Massachusetts Legislature that the Betterment Act was passed in 1808, by which squatters who had lived on land acquired by speculators or others for six years could not be evicted and could obtain title to the land on payment of its value before it was cleared. This was to be paid within a year. The value of their improvement was to be fixed by a jury of men from the neighborhood. If the land reverted to the proprietor, he had to pay the squatter for his improvement of the land. This act was naturally popular in the District of Maine, and as a large landowner in the District who wanted to attract settlers, King was anxious to protect their claims.

One of King's first settlers on his Million Acre Farm was a member of the surveying party, Solomon Stanley of Winthrop, who liked the land so well that he went there to live in 1807. He built the first dam on the Carrabassett River to furnish power for a gristmill, sawmill, and dyehouse for the settlement he established. King bought these later and added a carding mill, potash mill, flour mill, and tannery. King also built a house for himself in Kingfield in 1821, to which he and Ann and the children could come. A plaque now marks the location.

J. F. Anderson in his reminiscences of King, quotes Deane Dudley of Kingfield:

> It is now twenty-eight years since I first saw that remarkable man, and yet his aspect, and even the very expression of his face are as vivid in my memory as the day when my childhood made his acquaintance. I was but a lad of seven years, and he was at least sixty-five. His large frame and heavy voice seemed too gigantic, just my ideal of a real governor of the old school. In fact, I never read or hear of a *governor* but *he* rises up before my mental vision... . The sound of his voice seemed to echo grimly from the deep concaves of his eyes, which, from under their forest-like brows, would sternly look a command, that was not to be resisted by ordinary mortals....
>
> Such was my first and last impression of him. He was not a minute observer of details, but a great generalizer. It is quite certain he had an eye to the causes and effects of things....[1]

Dudley commented that King did not notice those around him or follow their actions when caring for his horses; also that he wanted everything written down, and trusted no matters to his memory. He liked one particular room in his house and wanted it thoroughly cleaned, no flies, or he would take charge and strike down the flies himself. His little girl was sick and subject to fits, but his ten-year-old son loved to play in the fields with the other boys and tell them about his studies. He had a little touch of aristocracy in his heart and was gentle, kind, and an artist.

According to Dudley, who evidently admired King, William liked to be called General King. He liked to eat the products of his farm when he arrived in Kingfield after driving there with his family in his big carriage.

One writer, John H. Sheppard, of Boston, Massachusetts, who recognized King's faults and the reason he also had enemies, notes, "In a brief sentence, his character may be summed up: if riding out on horseback for pleasure, he met a beggar asking alms, he would relieve him in a moment; but let him be in hot haste after some distance object, the grand old General would ride over that very mendicant, nor cast a lingering look behind. . . ."[2]

In 1808, King had acquired the most notable of his real estate properties, a farm just north of Bath on the Whiskeag Hill. Now known as the Stonehouse, it may have been built by King or some Englishmen who wanted a hunting lodge. There is an unverified story that it was built to resemble a church to prevent attack in case an enemy sighted it from the river. The main house has a very long sloping roof, and its windows and door are arched in the Gothic manner. The cathedral windows extend to and light the second story, while the third story is lighted by dormers. There is an attic above this with stairs leading to a cupola. The house is a fine example of eighteenth-century construction, solidly built, with walls made entirely of granite blocks, many of them twenty inches thick; there are no sills. It would have been a good fortress in those days. The cellar beams are fourteen inches square, with joists carefully mortised into them. The wooden floor and roof were put together entirely with wooden pegs. The heavy granite blocks were quarried on the place and the remains of the quarry can still be seen. It is thought that the timbers used in the foundation and roof were also found on the farm. In the month of October 1809, King is said to have bought of Low & Co. at the foot of Center Street hill, 14,700 bricks. These could have been to use in enlarging his home at the Point, or it is possible he planned to use the Stonehouse in case of war and needed them there.

The mystery of who built the Stonehouse was not solved by searching the deeds in Wiscasset Courthouse, though numerous purchases and sales of land were found dating back to 1802 and 1803 among King's real estate transactions in Bath, Georgetown, West Bath, Topsham, Litchfield, and Thomaston. Joshua Shaw sold him the land from Vine Street to Elm Street in 1803, where he had his dock. He bought Line's Island in the Kennebec from Mr. Gardiner that same year. All of these transactions were for lumber and farm products for King's trade. He raised apples and potatoes as well as livestock on the Stonehouse farm.

Later, in 1820 and 1822, King acquired the land, wharf, and store from the Knox property in Thomaston, and added the lime business to his trade.

V

POLITICAL parties and war at home and abroad had an increasing effect on King's business and life during these turbulent times. During Washington's administration two political parties emerged with different opinions of how to run the government of the new nation. Alexander Hamilton became the leader of the Federalists, who were mostly from old, well-known families with money and influence. They believed in a strong central government and were staunch supporters of the Constitutional Convention in Philadelphia. They generally favored Great Britain in her war with France. William's brothers Rufus and Cyrus were Federalists and William first supported this party, until he became disillusioned with the Federalists in Boston over their treatment of the District of Maine.

The anti-Federalists included a large number of farmers, laborers, and shopkeepers, as well as most of the pioneers in the West. They feared too much power in the central government and felt that the Federalists would not share all the benefits of the new form of government with them.

Adams, who followed Washington as President, was a Federalist. He kept the United States out of war, but there was much dissatisfaction over his foreign policies. The anti-Federalists joined a newly formed political party, the Democrat-Republicans, under the leadership of Thomas Jefferson, who was elected in 1801. William King, who admired and was friendly with Jefferson, believed in his policies and joined his party. He supported him and Madison, who followed Jefferson in 1809. King had great hopes that his party would supply leadership that would benefit the United States and his District.

The war between Great Britain and France had been renewed in 1803 and caused an increased need of lumber and provisions for the two countries. This encouraged King, on March 1, 1804, to join the Maine merchants Peleg Tallman, Abiel Wood, and Moses Carleton in a partnership with John Frazier and John Savage of Boston, which was to last four years.

King now shared three business locations with Dr. Benjamin Jones Porter in Topsham; he was in business in Bath with Peter Green in his store and with Bosworth in the shipyard; he had banking duties in the Wiscasset bank; and the Marine Insurance Company in Boston kept him in that city part of the time. From Ann's letters to him we learn that she was keeping in touch with his business in Bath, but was not happy to have him away from home so much.

Troublesome years began in 1807 when Napoleon turned against all trading of neutrals with Great Britain. He had failed to take Great Britain, so he turned on Austria and Russia, who had been supporting her, and began the conquest of the Continent. Because of Britain's success against the French fleet, Britain had become "mistress of the seas." Napoleon, believing Great Britain's strength lay in her commerce, determined to ruin her by excluding her goods from France and all other states of Europe under his control. On May 16, 1807, although his fleet was too weak to enforce it, he issued a decree declaring that the British Isles were in a state of blockade, and he threatened to seize the ships of any country that traded with them. Great Britain then replied by Orders in Council, threatening to seize any ships trading with France and her allies. This of course included neutrals and was a threat to King and his associates and their chartered business.

King's first loss under the Orders in Council came that same year. The brig *Fair American,* owned by him and Robert Harding, was seized by the British brig *Scout,* on suspicion of carrying French property, and taken to Gibraltar thirty-five days after leaving Baltimore. Captain Harding and his crew were released, but there is no account of the return of the brig and cargo.

The British did not stop at taking American vessels. Short of seamen, British navy captains stopped United States merchant vessels and searched them for deserters. In those days sailors who came to America found better conditions on American vessels, and many took out naturalization papers. The British government did not recognize their right to do this: "Once an Englishman always an Englishman," they declared. They found it hard to tell an American from an Englishman and took many Americans in spite of proof of birth and the protests of United States citizens. Sailors on William King's vessels carried these proofs and were fortunate not to be impressed into the British Navy, for there would have been little chance of their ever being allowed to leave.

Even United States navy ships were not safe from abuse. An incident off the Virginia coast in 1807 brought to the attention of Americans the contemptuous and high-handed treatment the British were giving our sailors and the United States naval vessels. A British squadron lost a number of men by desertion and had reason to believe that the ringleader, Jenkin Ratford, had enlisted aboard the United States frigate *Chesapeake* under Commander Barron. When the British frigate *Leopard* signaled "dispatches," Commander Barron, unaware of Ratford's presence aboard and thinking the British wanted some mail sent, backed his topsail and invited the Captain to send a boat out. The dispatches turned out to be an order from Admiral Berkley of the British squadron to search the American frigate for deserters. Barron replied that the only so-called deserters in his crew were three Americans who had formerly been impressed; and that he would not permit the search.

The boarding party left and about eight minutes later, the *Leopard* fired her full broadside into the *Chesapeake,* and poured two more before Barron could reply, for the *Chesapeak's* decks had been littered with stores and few of her guns were mounted. After suffering the killing of three and the wounding of eighteen of his crew, Barron struck the flag. His crew were then mustered on deck and Ratford

and the three Americans were taken off by the *Leopard's* officers.*
The American frigate was then allowed to limp back to Norfolk.
This insult to our navy vessel and the brutal treatment of our men
made Americans angry. In addition to this, people on the western
frontier believed the British were inciting the Indians to attack their
settlements.

It was hard for William King and other New England traders who
had had good relations with British businessmen to believe that the
British government supported this treatment of United States
sailors and navy vessels. King felt that President Jefferson's
recommendation of an embargo might solve their problem, and he
was in agreement with Congress when they passed the Embargo
Act of 1807. This Act forbade any American vessel to clear from an
American harbor for a foreign port and placed coasting vessels and
fishing boats under heavy bonds not to land their cargoes outside
the United States. Another act at the same time forbade the
importation of British goods.

Confident that the French and British would soon revoke their
decree and it would not be long before his ships would sail again,
William determined to build some larger vessels to add to his fleet.
He would prepare for an upsurge of business as soon as the Embargo
had lifted. Men were out of-work in Bath and their families were
suffering. He could give them work at low wages only, but it would
tide them over until better times came. In 1807 King had his largest
vessel, the *Resolution,* 353 tons burthen, built. This was followed in
1808 by the brigs *Perserverance,* 235 tons, and *Harmony,* 194 tons.
He also in that same year bought one-half interest in the *Latonia,*
renamed the *Margaretta.*

King was serving as senator from Lincoln County in the
Massachusetts General Court in 1807 and 1808. Traveling between
Boston and Bath, often by stage, he became appalled at the hardship
the Embargo was imposing on the people. In the District of Maine
some merchants had resorted to smuggling to save their businesses.
Others like himself had tied up their vessels. At Bath there were
sixteen ships and twenty-seven brigs, amounting to 9,000 tons of

---

* Ratford was hanged and the three Americans were impressed into the British Navy again.

cargo space, besides a number of schooners and sloops tied up to wharves or anchored in the river; of these King had the ships *Reserve, Resolution, Vigilant, Reunion,* and *United States,* and the brigs *Huron* and *Harmony,* all laden and ready for departure, also the brig *Valarius,* not loaded — 2,475 tons in all. He figured he was losing about $5,558 a month, exclusive of interest on his money and cargoes. Over-extended merchants were losing their businesses by 1808. So far, King was holding his own. The Embargo was not working out as he had hoped it would.

Letters from King's agents in Liverpool and London informed him of their friendship, quoting prices for merchandise and needed supplies. They gave him assurances of business as soon as the Embargo was lifted, but no indication that the British were hurt by it, or that the government would rescind the Orders in Council.

In 1806 the federal government had built a fort at the mouth of the Kennebec on Hunnewell's Point. It was under the direction of the Collector of Customs. A government-owned cutter was sent there to enforce the Embargo. Rebellious men who regarded the Embargo as an invasion of their rights as free men defied the government whenever they could. One of these men, John Richardson, of Bath, sent his vessel, the *Sally,* with his son William as supercargo to London with a load of lumber. They ran the gauntlet of the fort, escaping with only a hole shot in her topsail and some of her rigging cut. The sale of the lumber she carried, it was said, formed the foundation of the fortune of William Richardson, who afterward married William King's niece, Harriet Leland. William King, however, made no effort to send his vessels to sea. He took the time to take Ann to New York and visit his brother Rufus and family. There he had a chance to discuss the situation with Rufus.

On his return home from New York, King determined to do something to lift the Embargo. He contacted his representative in the United States Congress and pointed out the District of Maine's desperate economic need to have the Embargo lifted. He had a meeting with Peleg Tallman, Moses Carleton, and Abiel Wood of Wiscasset and they sent a letter giving the views of Maine's leading merchants for Orchard Cook of Wiscasset to present to Congress.

GENERAL WILLIAM KING

In the letter they stated that they believed the Embargo should be raised, with no half measures. A non-intercourse bill would not help them because their business was chiefly with England and France, and Maine lumbermen would be hurt by it. As for doing business through Spain and Portugal, they thought it should not be considered, especially as Napoleon would probably take over these countries. Armed vessels could lead to war. If the Embargo should last beyond March 1, 1809, they predicted the federal government might be in peril of the separation of states, because it would create organized opposition to federal law.

King kept in constant communication with Orchard Cook and Joseph F. Wingate, of Bath, about the debate in Congress over the Embargo. Cook promised he would do all in his power to rouse Congress to the need of abolishing the Embargo Act, but he warned King that there were other states with other interests angry over the treatment our country was receiving from both Britain and France; the District of Maine was not the only part of the country to be considered. He believed, however, that the Embargo would be lifted by March 1, 1809, in view of the sentiment of Congress, but thought they might have a compromise in a non-intercourse bill. This happened as he predicted: Congress rescinded the Embargo on March 1, 1809, but on the same day they passed the Non-intercourse Bill, allowing trade with all but England and France. New England merchants were not happy over this.

President Madison, hoping to do something to ease the situation, consulted the British minister, who assured him that the British government would soon repeal the Orders in Council. Madison, pleased with the assurance, rescinded the Non-intercourse Law on April 19, 1809. King, one of the first to receive the good news, released his vessels for trade. On June 14, 1809, he had seven or eight of them in Liverpool, unloading or waiting to be unloaded.

When the President learned that the minister had misinformed him and that the British government had no intention of repealing the Orders in Council, he reimposed the Non-intercourse law, in August. This change of policy made it difficult for American merchants in distant ports and difficult for owners to get in touch with their captains. Coasting laws were strict, too. Frazier, King's business associate in Boston, wrote to him not to let the *Reunion* go coasting, because, should they try to trade illegally, costly bonds on the trade might cause them to pay heavy fines.

It was said that under the Non-intercourse law some of King's captains took advantage of him and traded illegally. They sold cargoes in forbidden ports and kept the proceeds, knowing that King could be blamed for it if they were caught. Angry because they did not follow his instructions, King had duplicate letters written instructing his captains where and what he wanted them to trade. He made them read the letters back to him and sign their names to both copies, of which he kept one in his files and gave the other to the captain to carry on board with him.

One of the incidents later charged to King concerned the *Alexander*, owned jointly by King, John Ring, and John O. Page of Hallowell, Captain Ballard, master. The *Alexander* had been tied up in Baltimore during the Embargo. After costly repairs, necessary because of her long period of inaction, she was put back into commission and service again.

The mate, Nathaniel Ripley, some years later gave testimony that on May 15, 1809 (during the shortlived lifting of the Non-intercourse law), the *Alexander* took a cargo of tobacco and white oak staves to Norfolk, Virginia. Then, on the twenty-first of June, the vessel sailed for London, but off Beachy Head in the English Channel, she was taken by a French privateer. The crew were taken aboard the privateer as prisoners, and she and her prize were anchored off the coast of Dieppe where they were attacked during the night by an English sloop-of-war, which succeeded in capturing the *Alexander*. The privateer escaped with the American prisoners still aboard.

The complete story of the *Alexander* was not given in the testimony and the question of illegal trading depended upon the point of view of those involved. King learned from his agents in England that the American seamen were put into prison by the French privateers and kept on a diet of bread and water in an attempt to force them to serve on board the privateer. Finally they were released by a man in Paris, who learned of their plight, furnished them with money, and enabled them to leave the country on a ship evacuating Americans.

In the meantime the British gunboat *Dapper* took the *Alexander* into Portsmouth, England, and she was transferred to London, where Captain Ballard with some of the crew took her back. There was much financial exchange, between salvage, insurance company, and payment to the agents in England; and the loss was shared by King, Ring and Page.

William King and his associates were not the only ones confused by the laws and war conditions. There was so much complaint that Madison and his Congress, hoping to get better terms for neutrals, passed the Macon Act, May 1, 1810, which restored commercial intercourse with both Britain and France, but offered to the first power that recognized neutral rights the bait of refusing to trade with her enemy. In the event of either country exempting the United States from its edicts, the President was authorized to forbid Americans trading with the other . . . provided the other did not follow suit within three months. This was to further complicate trading.

The British, too, had laws that were complicated. Porter & King, in order to trade with England, had to submit to a law that Americans could not trade with the French or French dependencies unless they paid duty in British ports and took out a license to trade. This was made less humiliating for them by their British agents, who made arrangements for charter voyages. Both countries needed certain products and allowed such trading. The partners' ships were making profits under British licenses, though some resented it, and many Americans were growing more angry over continued impressment of our seamen and insulting treatment of our navy.

In spite of their confusion and the threat of war with either France or England, the years 1809 through 1812 were busy ones for Porter & King and their Boston associates. Their fleet was making money, though at times relations with the British were strained. On July eighth, Captain James Oliver wrote to King from Liverpool, where he was discharging cargo from the *United States,* that on the morning of July fourth all of the American ships in port had displayed their colors, but that in the afternoon a mob had swarmed aboard the vessels, torn down the flags, and carried them away, in many instances dragging them in the streets. Luckily the Americans had made no attempt at resistance, and thus no one was killed. The

Mayor of Liverpool had called out his force in the evening and cleared the streets of the rioters.

Though the British man in the street evidently resented the display of patriotism by Americans, businessmen were still prepared to trade with them.

Later King & Porter found that the French were not disposed to treat American traders any better. In 1810, King's nephew, Captain Richard Porter, was master of the *United States*. In a letter to his uncle, dated March 10, he wrote that a severe gale of wind that lasted four days had driven about thirty vessels ashore on the coast of France, they were taken possession of by the French and set afire. There were eight American vessels among them, all burned. (The only one from the Kennebec region was the ship *Commoner*.)

In July 1810, Napoleon had all American merchantmen in port seized and he ordered by imperial command the sale of all ships and cargoes. On the same day he told the American minister that he loved Americans and because of that he was revoking his decrees against them, it being understood that the British were going to revoke theirs. Napoleon by this stroke of diplomacy took advantage of the Macon Act to push Americans toward war with Great Britain, for the British stubbornly refused to revoke their Orders in Council or to acknowledge the Americans as neutrals. It would be of interest to know what King's comments were on this state of affairs, for it directly affected his business with the English agents in London and Liverpool.

King learned that there was some advantage to the Act for American trade. On January 10, 1810, his commission agent in Savannah, Georgia, wrote that King's ship the *United States,* had arrived in port and several freights had been offered Captain Porter but did not meet with the captain's approval. He was waiting, for a great number of English ships were there and in their extreme anxiety to load and get away before the first of February, when the Macon Act went into effect, they had caused the price of lumber to advance to the enormous sum of $412.50 per thousand feet, and lumber even at that price was scarce. After February, the agent thought, the English vessels not being admitted, the captain would have no trouble getting freight at reasonable prices and carrying it to England, as American vessels were not barred from English ports.

The *Reserve* was at Savannah at this time, taking on a load of cotton. Laborers were scarce and they had to depend upon the crew to load. When the *Reserve* arrived in Liverpool, they received a cool welcome. The commission merchant wrote to King telling him of the vessel's arrival and adding that on account of the enforcement of the Orders in Council, he could not tell whether he would be able to obtain return freight for her.

He also notified King of the arrival of the *Ann* and the *Reunion* and said he hoped they would be allowed to discharge their cargoes. Relations were becoming so strained that businessmen on both sides were being hurt. King became more cautious in trading in the West Indies and insisted upon the procedure of duplicate signed letters of instruction for his captains, as shown in the following letters to Captain Foote of the brig *Huron* and Captain Prior of the ship *Reserve:*

Bath, Dec 13, 1811

Capt David Foote,
Sir the Brig Huron being now loaded with a cargo of lumber you will proceed the first favourable wind for the Island of Dominica, where you will dispose of your cargo to the best advantage, you will by allmeans collect the amt. you have formally left there even should you have to go to any other Island for a part of your payment but this you must avoid if possible. —

You will take a Clearance as from St. Bartholomew and get a Certificate likewise of the Origin signed by two merchants of that place purporting that it is the groth and produce of that Island.

This I presume you will be able to do without gowing down with your Vessel —

You will write frequently and give me particularly the State of your business —

Wishing you a fair wind and safe return I remain Respectfully Yours —

Signed, William King

Bath, April 8, 1812

Capt. Mathew Prior,
Sir,

The Ship Reserve being now loaded with a Cargo of Lumber, Fish, Flour, et, et. as per Invoice enclosed you will proceed the first Wind for the Island of Martinica, where should you not feel assured of doing better at some other place, you will dispose of your Cargo, as you are prepared for takeing home Molasses I should recommend your takeing that article in payment.

I hope you will be quite particular as to the person you dispose of your Cargo to, and by all means to make your bargain that the payment will be made you as fast as you can take it in, as it will be important for you to be away in thirty days at furthest (?) from the time you make your entry —

The Fish is of a most excellent quality and I really hope you will be able to get a very good price for it.

You will enquire of Mr. _____ (?) whether the ballance was received from Pitcher by Capt. Lane, should it be the case that he has left any part of that debt behind you will take care to obtain it and bring it home with you if possible —

Should their be permission when you arrive at Martinice to export Sugar and Coffee in American Vessels to this Country, you would do well to take about one thousand dollars in Coffee, alike amount in Sugar, but not to do it unless there is permission, you will do well to be quite particular not in any instance to contravene any Law, Custom of Usage in the transacting of your business —

For your better encouragement during the present Voyage I shall allow you twenty five dollars per month as wages, and five per cent on what you bring home, the proceeds of the present Cargo

So wishing you a fine wind and an expeditious Voyage, I remain as Usual —

Signed, William King

I acknowledge to have received a Copy of the above orders —
(signed) Matw Prior

VI

WHEN the Embargo was imposed on shipping and the Nonintercourse Law followed it, Massachusetts authorities had turned against the Republican party (the prefix Democrat had been dropped) because these acts interfered with their trade with Great Britain and other foreign countries. Blaming the Republicans in power in Washington, they turned to the Federalist party again. The District of Maine, however, where citizens believed Massachusetts favored large landowners, had supported the Republicans and elected William King as senator from Lincoln County to the General Court in 1807.

Diplomatic relations with Great Britain had not improved in 1808, and Camden and other towns along the Maine coast, many of which had not forgotten the brutal treatment they had received from the British in the Revolution, petitioned Massachusetts for some assistance for their defense in case of war, stressing their military needs of men, guns, ammunition, and provisions.

Massachusetts authorities reluctantly decided they must prepare to defend the eastern coast. The General Court of the Commonwealth of Massachusetts, still largely Republican at this time, commissioned William King as major-general, on March 8,

1808, to command the Eleventh Division of militia. This consisted of four regiments in the District of Maine. King had no military training other than previous service in the militia, yet he was to serve with credit in the war to come. When he returned from Boston after his appointment, he was met by troops from Topsham, Brunswick, and Bath and escorted into town. He was justly proud of his title and uniform and preferred the title of General after this. He at once began the study of military information and procedure and consulted his friends in military service in preparation for his new duties.

He was not surprised on June 18, 1812, after an embargo of ninety days, that war was declared against Great Britain. He had seen it coming. He had learned from his friends in Congress of the ambitious plans of the "war hawks" to invade Canada. Of these he did not approve. He knew that many Americans had a right to be angry over the impressment of more than six thousand United States seamen into the British navy and that navy's insults to the United States flag and navy vessels. His business had suffered, too, under the Orders in Council. In spite of the fact that his agents in England remained friendly, he saw that it was time to prepare to protect and defend his state and nation from further injury.

Local defense was chiefly up to the militia, the towns appropriating part of the pay and equipment and the state the remainder. Most of the federal forces were soon employed on the extensive land frontier of the states. The wartime quota for the militia was 100,000 in the states, and the District of Maine's quota was 2,500.

When King set out to organize the defenses of Lincoln County he was in command of the local troops and had some able and experienced officers on whom he could depend. At home, General Denny McCobb's first brigade under Colonel Andrew Reed consisted of the North Company under Captain Benjamin Davenport, and the South Company under Captain John Pettis. The Light Infantry was under Captain William Torry. These troops were supported by Brunswick regiments under Major Holden and Captain Abel Boynton. A small company of troops were at the fort at Popham under Captain John Wilson of Topsham, supported by some militiamen under federal pay. In addition to the above, Captain Horatio G. Allen, Lieutenant James McClellan, and Ensign C. Waterman, of Bath, formed a company of townsmen who were too old or too young to be in the militia. They had no uniforms, but drilled and prepared to help defend Bath in an emergency. Adjutant Zina Hyde assisted King, and Reverend William Jenks was chaplain.

Toward the east, Camden had a similar organization with Colonel Erastus Foote in command of the fifth regiment. Each town along the coast called town meetings and made plans to defend themselves against possible invasion. King used his lovely home in Bath for his headquarters, but Wiscasset was the place of meeting when the Major-General issued orders for the whole division to appear in arms. At home he entertained his officers and made plans for the District.

King and his merchant friends had not wanted war. They knew that the United States government did not have the required number of men trained for the army. King's position as defender of Lincoln County's coast under Federalist Massachusetts was made more difficult by Governor Strong's opposition to the war and his defiance of the War Department when he refused to allow the government to employ any of the Massachusetts militia. The War Department, when refused help, withdrew most of its troops manning United States garrisons in Massachusetts and Maine, leaving a few of their less competent men there. Massachusetts and the District of Maine were left with only the militia to defend the coast against a powerful enemy.

In great need of volunteers for his army, United States General Dearborn turned to King in a letter written on July 20, 1812 asking him to help raise a brigade of volunteers for the army that had just been authorized by Congress and remarking that no man could raise a brigade in the state as quickly as he could.

King replied to General Dearborn's letter, explaining his position, consulted the Secretary of War, William Eustis, and accepted the challenge to superintend the raising and organizing of companies of volunteers. As soon as it was known that King was recruiting, his mail was full of letters asking for officer's commissions and positions as surgeons and chaplains. He was busy answering questions about pay, organization of companies, and equipment needed. He made frequent trips throughout the District and to Boston. Muster rolls, payrolls, and lists of equipment passed through King's office, as well as complaints that needed remedy. These were passed on to the proper authorities after he okayed them.

Dearborn's faith in his friend's ability to raise volunteer troops paid off. Williamson writes: "... a greater number of soldiers was recruited for the army, in this District, according to its population, than in any one of the States."[4] Enlistments were brisk in some of the towns, and companies of troops were raised in Portland, Kennebunk, Phippsburg, Castine, and Eastport. While these men were organizing and training, King had to depend upon his militia in their home towns. Citizens were alerted and watching the sea for British ships and the hated Tory "shaving mills,"* an added hazard for the small merchant and fishing vessels. Companies of militia organized and drilled to protect their towns. King ordered their officers to use their own judgment for defense when an alarm was sounded, sending for him and reserves when needed.

Massachusetts authorities were not very happy about King's activities in raising volunteers for the U.S. Army. In June 1813 he received a letter from Samuel Putnam, questioning his position and motives. King replied, keeping a duplicate of his answer in his files, as follows:

Bath June 21, 1813.

Sir,

Your letter as chairman of a joint Committee of the Legislature of Massachusetts I received this day. In answer to your enquiry whether I hold any Military Commission under the President of the U.S., I answer, that I have not the honour of holding any such Commission; I am not insensible however at a crisis like the present,

---

* Shallow Nova Scotia craft, with open decks, carrying sails and sweeps and manned by six or eight armed men. These boats could dart in and out of small rivers and creeks and make swift captures of coasters and fishermen. They were extremely difficult to catch.

to hold a Commission under an office so determined to protect the right and uphold the character of our Country, must be flattering to any American.

You also desire to be informed if I have accepted any agency or concern under the U. States in relation to the distribution of arms or enlisting or organizing any Soldiers for the service of the U. States, or for Commissioning officers for the Service? To which I reply that I have not had any agency or concern in relation to the distribution of Arms. — With respect to the arms that have been distributed in this District, — The Volunteers that tendered their services to the President, for the defence of the Country, and have been accepted and organized, have been furnished with arms on application to the proper officers of the Gen'l Government. —

As it respects organizing soldiers for the service of the U. States, I have much pleasure in stating, that soon after the commencement of the present war, when the services of the detached militia of this State was withheld from the General Government, I aided the war department in organizing such a Volunteer military force, as was considered necessary for the defence of this District, the commissions to the officers was passed through my hands for that purpose; this I did without any promise of Compensation on their part, or any expectation or desire on mine to accept of any. —

As the Legislature will no doubt be advised of the result of your enquiry, and as I presume you will be much gratified in availing yourself of the present opportunity of doing Justice to the Patriotism of the people in this District, it is with real satisfaction that I state to you for their information that after two Regts, of Volunteers were organized, which was all that was considered necessary for the defence of this District, the services of such a number of other Companies were tendered to the President, and not accepted as would have completed three Regts more had they been wanted.

Believing that a War in defence of the personal liberty of our Seamen, a class of our fellow citizens that have so recently, and so repeatedly proved to their Country that they so well deserve it — to be just and necessary, I have in conclusion Gentlemen only to request you to be assured, that as a Citizen of the U. States I have duties to perform, as well as those of a Citizen of this State, and while I shall endeavour not to neglect the latter, the former will most unquestionably be attended to. —

> I am Gentlemen Respectfully
> Your Ob. Servant —
> *Wm. King*[2]

Hon. Saml. Putnam
Chairman of a
Joint Committee of
the Legislature

For the defense of eastern Maine and under General Dearborn's directions, King had two companies of militia detached from General Blake's brigade on the Penobscot and stationed at Fort Sullivan in Eastport under Major Philip Ulmer, to prevent smuggling and any illicit dealings with the enemy. Within a year they were relieved by volunteer troops under Colonel Commandant George Ulmer, Esq. From him King received numerous complaints. The regular troops did not welcome him, he lacked food, shelter, and equipment for his troops, and had no money to pay them. In addition, British vessels blocked Ulmer from getting supplies by sea, and land transportation was slow and inadequate. Forced to borrow from citizens to pay his bills, he incurred their wrath by his attempts to prevent smuggling. He began drinking heavily in his frustration, lost the respect of his men, and was finaly thrown in jail for not repaying his loans. William Stern, who sympathized with Ulmer, wrote to King about the situation and sent him the facts by Captain Spear. He advised King to try to "discharge Ulmer in a delicate way for the benefit of all." This was done in such a way that Ulmer continued a friend of King. They then sent Major Perley Putnam, of Salem, to take his place. At this time there were seventy men in the fort and thirty men stationed in Robbinston, hardly enough to face even a small number of British invaders.

At the beginning of the war, King continued trading for needed supplies and for his family's comfort, in spite of the threat of British warships patrolling off the coast. It was important to the people of

GENERAL WILLIAM KING   49

Bath and surrounding towns to obtain supplies by sea because land transportation was still very poor. King relied on British licenses or neutral Swedish vessels to import English goods.

Some of the British commanders did not take the defense measures of the Americans very seriously. Perhaps they hoped the New England states would separate from the other states and return to the rule of the mother country. There is a traditional story handed down through the family of Joshua Marston, coachman and general helper for King, that a British commander, perhaps trading on a past acquaintance, sent word to the General that he would come upriver and take supper with him. As acting commander of defense, King was not disposed to treat such a suggestion lightly. He sent back word that if the British commander came he "would take supper in Hell." King was willing to get needed supplies from British sources, but not to socialize with the enemy.

It was during these years that King stored extra supplies in his warehouse, for he feared a tightening of the blockade already threatening the towns to the east. A letter to King, dated 25 November 1812, shows that he was also looking out for his family's comfort.

> Honorable Wm. King
>   According to your Order I have shipped on Board the Sch. *Saucy Jack* Capt. McKown Bound to Bath. the Articles of furniture you were pleased to Engage Which hopes will Come Safe to hand anexed is the Acct. which will Vary a Little from the Estimate gave But is as Low as Can be furnished.
>   The Eastimate of the Cornices were made for painted white & gold. But Experience teaches me will not Last more than 2 years & appear Decent. those Gilt & Burni (rest of the word covered with seal) and will with Care Last 20 years — taking Care not to wipe them with a wet Cloath &c. and Only Costs 5 Doll's Extra-
>   When the Bedstead is put up have the Tester put together the Dimity for which is Longer than the head Cloath & for the Latter there is a Drapery inside to Correspond with the foot the Other draperes are so tacked that I think there Can be no mistake in puting up I Could not match the Dimity for the Counterpane nearer than that Sent and Cost me 60 Cts pry. I have had the Cash

to pay for nearly All the Meterials and hopes you will Remit the Amt. of the Acct. by Return of post and Oblidge

your most Obt. Sevt
Willm. LeMON

P.S. it is Said the British privateer. Liverpool packet was off marblehead yesterday. it remains with you to make insurance. or not. as they are at your Risk. [3]

There is no record that King lost his bedstead or any of his orders from Boston at this time, for the British were protecting and helping New England traders in 1812, needing their goods and trade. Before the Non-importation Act went into effect, a number of American vessels, whose owners had been profitably engaged in trade with the Iberian Peninsula, hastened to Lisbon with cargoes for the allied British and Spanish armies; and Britain, needing supplies, promptly took steps to encourage such trade, even in the face of war declared by the United States. The plan of issuing "British licenses" to American vessels engaged in this trade had developed, it was stated, so that the possession of such licenses would exempt a United States owned vessel from seizure by a British naval cruiser or privateer, despite the fact that the two countries were at war. A letter and report of Captain Joshua Barney, master of the American privateer *Rossie*, reveals that William King's vessels were engaged in this trade. Captain Barney was indignant and reported his frustration after capturing the *Nymph* of Newburyport. He wrote to his contact in Washington:

> The first vessel I fell in with was an *American* from *Martinique* bound to Bath (U.S.) his cargo, *molasses, the produce of that island* certified under the hand and seal of the *British* Governor. After examining him strictly *(under English colors)* and obtained all the information I could, I informed him, I was an *American,* as such should send him in for a breach of the non-importation law, he then produced *Spanish* clearances from *Porto Rico* and insisted he was from that port, however, I ordered the vessel into port. After I had taken possession of his vessel, he informed me that a ship then in sight was also from Martinique. In consequence I gave chase and came up with her, she showed me a clearance also (forged) from *Porto Rico* and denied having come from Martinique, but on examining his papers, I found every proof of the fact except the

Governor's pass, being under English colors. I examined his manifest and there appeared on the face of it a report of only *one half* of it, for his entry into the U.S. I asked him how he could get over making a report of only one half of his cargo on arrival. He said it was the usual mode (carried over from colonial days). That they never entered more than the half. I then demanded what he would do in case of seizure, his answer was, that his ship belongs to *General William King*, that no person dared to seize her, if he did Mr. *Madison* was a friend of Mr. King and would order her release. (I also questioned the other captain the same way, he also informed me, that "everybody" to the eastward acted in the same manner.) After I had learnt all I could I informed him that he had violated laws of his country in a twofold degree. Firstly by a breach of the non-importation law and secondly by a breach of the revenue law and that I should make a prize of him. He then threatened me with the power and standing of his owner. I knew General W. King to be what is called a good Democrat and friendly to the executive. I considered such a seizure at this time would be made a handle by the enemies of the administration and I released him, fully determined to give you the above information. During the time I acted the Englishman with the Americans, I found out that the Revenue was defrauded by the eastern men without ceremony. They introduced large cargoes of drygoods from the enemies ports which are *run* in *without* duties.[4]

King, as other merchants of New England, was following the practice of their colonial predecessors. British goods imported through Halifax and St. John, New Brunswick, and owned by citizens of the United States were also protected by the British for a while. All they feared were United States privateers. Massachusetts authorities, not in favor of the war that hurt their business, cooperated with the British, and there was much smuggling across the northern border of the District of Maine, and also in Florida, which the United States government was finding hard to stop.

In 1813 King's business associate and sometimes political rival, Peleg Tallman, was appointed Swedish Vice-Council for the District of Maine in charge of so-called neutral trade. Trade increased in vessels flying the Swedish flags after this. British goods were getting scarce and neutral vessels could import goods into Bath legally. It seems reasonable to believe that King, Peter Green, and

William Emerson registered their brig, the *Margaretta*, built in Newburyport in 1813, under Swedish colors at this time. King had a half interest in her. In doing this King and his associates unwittingly brought war closer to Lincoln County. Henry Owen, in his *History of Bath*, quotes a letter sent to Captain Preble from Charles Tappan of Cambridge that explains how the *Margaretta* brought war closer to Bath and the surrounding towns:

> At the commencement of our war with Great Britain in 1812, the United States had but few if any factories for the manufacture of woolen cloths and blankets and the soldiers were clad in British cloths and slept under British blankets. It was understood that no captures would be made of British goods owned by citizens of the United States, and many American merchants imported, via Halifax and St. John, N.B., their usual stock of goods. In 1813 I went with others in the Swedish brig *Margaretta*, to St. John, N.B., and filled her with British goods, intending to take them to Bath, Me., and enter them regularly and pay the lawful duties thereon. All we had to fear was American privateers; and we hired Captain Blyth of H.B.M. brig *Boxer*, to convoy us to the mouth of the Kennebec River, for which service we gave him a bill of exchange on London for £100. We sailed in company, and in a thick fog off Quoddy Head, the Boxer took us in tow. It was agreed that when we were about to enter the mouth of the river, two or three guns should be fired over us, to have the appearance of trying to stop us, should any idle folks be looking on. Capt. Burroughs, of the U.S. brig Enterprise, lay in Portland harbor, and hearing the guns got underway, and as is well known, captured the Boxer after a severe engagement, in which both captains were killed. Our bill of exchange we thought might get us into trouble, and we employed Esquire K. to take 500 specie dollars on board the captured ship and exchange them for the paper, which was found in Capt. Blyth's breeches pocket.[5]

On September 8, King received a letter from Amos Piper, of Boothbay Harbor, giving him an eyewitness account of the battle that followed the *Margaretta's* entrance into the Kennebec. On January 4, 1814, King paid $20,000 to the customs collector, listing certain wares, goods, and merchandise entered by him and imported by the brig *Margaretta* from L.F. Roby, Port St. John, New Brunswick. This manifest shows the value of the goods Capt. Blyth was guarding for King and his partners. We wonder if King thought of the part he played in the presence of the *Boxer* off the coast when he heard the popular song written about the sea fights in the War of 1812, one verse of which was:

> Then next you sent your Boxer,
>   To box us all about,
> But we had an "enterprising" brig
>   That beat your Boxer out;
> We boxed her up to Portland,
>   And moored her off the town,
> To show the Sons of Liberty
>   The Boxer of renown.[6]

In November 1813, the British blockade tightened. President Madison, advised of the weakness of defense in eastern Maine, decided to nationalize a portion of the militia and authorized William King, whom he felt he could trust, to organize an expedition to defend the northeast part of the District. The government did not have money to finance the expedition, so General Dearborn, in charge of New England defense, ordered King to go to Governor Strong for a loan. Caught between the United States authorities and the Massachusetts governor, King made the request, only to be refused. Strong was not interested in his plans for the defense of northern Maine. Later King learned these plans were published in a Boston paper and the British were informed of them. This did not increase his faith in Massachusetts authorities. He felt that they were more concerned in promoting the Hartford Convention in order to humiliate the federal government than in defending Maine. Believing that Massachusetts authorities cared little for the fate of his district, King returned home determined to organized an expedition of his own.

The last of 1813 and the first of 1814 saw increased pressure by the British along the eastern coast. Britain, failing to make a separate peace with New England, declared a tight blockade and invasion of the District as far as the Penobscot Bay, claiming this part of the territory was a part of Canada. The British warships *Rattler* and *Bream* began patrolling from the Kennebec to the St. George's River and captured five schooners off Pemaquid. Boothbay men succeeded in recapturing one, then they called on old Captain Tucker to command a vessel to capture the *Bream*, which was harassing Bristol and the neighboring towns. Not finding the *Bream*, Tucker's little schooner encountered the British privateer *Crown* and captured it. This was a boon to the people along the coast, for they were out of provisions and the *Crown* was filled with provisions for the *Rattler*. King had the British prisoners jailed in Wiscasset and they were later exchanged for Americans. From this time on, King was receiving more demands for ammunition and equipment from the towns and was finding both hard to get.

The tight blockade ordered by the British government on April 25 was followed by an expedition against Eatport, where the United States forces were too weak to resist capture. One by one, Hampden, Castine, Machias, Bangor, Brewer, and other towns too ill-equipped and untrained to fight had to surrender to British rule. Oaths of allegiance to the British Crown were required, and most of the soldiers were paroled. No more smuggling took place after this.

The militia of Camden and neighboring towns were having a hard time trying to protect their shipping and homes from harassing British invaders when, on June 20, 1814, Samuel Sewall, on duty at the mouth of the Kennebec River, reported to Colonel Reed that a 74-gun man-o-war, flying British colors, was lying off Seguin Island and in the act of transferring a considerble force to barges lying alongside. The British captains did not attempt to enter the river, fearing the currents and damage to their big ships, but their barges were equipped with swivel guns. Colonel Reed, according to instructions, had the alarm gun at Phippsburg Center fired and sent young John Langdon Hill, son of Mark L. Hill, Paul-Revere style, to alert people along the road and to deliver the news to General King in Bath.

The General was in his office at the bank and on receiving the news, stuck his head out the window and shouted to the crowd below, "The enemy is coming! Every man arm, and to his alarm post instantly!"[7] He then sent Adjutant Zina Hyde to alert the town and call out the militia. Leaving General Denny McCobb to station his men in Bath, King rode to Phippsburg to learn more of the situation.

The men were soon stationed, and a period of anxious waiting for the British to appear was broken only by the Reverend Mr. Jenks,

GENERAL WILLIAM KING 55

who, urged by some timid townsmen, attempted to take a flag of truce downriver to prevent the destructionof the town. The militia objected and sent a boat after him and brought him back.

It is said the cash in the Lincoln Bank was removed in a nail keg to Peleg Tallman's farmhouse in Woolwich for fear it would be confiscated, for his friendship with the British would not prevent the plundering of his bank; now the mask of friendship was removed.

The British warship proved to be H.M.S. *Bulwark,* which sent barges up the Sheepscot, where they were driven off by the militia. On their way back, they were fired on from Pond Island. Discouraged by this show of defense, the British warship left.

Relieved that there was no further danger from the *Bulwark,* the people of Bath returned to their homes, but they were determined not to endure the abuse, plundering, burning of ships, and humiliation the towns to the east had suffered, and they petitioned King to have one hundred militiamen on duty all the time for the defense of the town. General King ordered General McCobb to detach this number from his brigade. A more detailed account of Major-General King's part in the attempted invasion was sent to General John Brooks in Boston; the duplicate, found in a drawer of an old table from King's home, is now owned by Jane Stevens, of Bath, who has generously given permission for its transcription here. It shows King's feelings about the lack of support he was receiving from Massachusetts:

> Sir, Referring His Excellency to my letter of the 21st in the morning for the occurencies previous to that time, I proceeded immediately after closing that letter to the U.S. post at the mouth of the River, there received information that the barges had been again sent off from the Bulwark and that they took a direction for Damariscotta, the ship was then under way and following in the same direction, being convinced that the Enemy had met with more opposition at the mouth of this River as well as on the Sheepscot, than they expected, and that there was no probability of their return, the Companies from Bath were ordered to return to that place. The Companies from Phippsburg then in the fort, as well as the Companies from Georgetown on the East side of the River were ordered to be discharged with the exception of a

detachment of 40 men from Phippsburg the Companies, that number having been requested by the Lieut't of the fort — They will remain in service and wate the order of the Commander in Chief, our Magistrate and the people generally being solitous that that should be the case. —

The troops assembled at Bath were discharged with the exception of the troops of the town on the evening of the 21st and those belonging to the town the next morning — The troops from Woolwich stationed at Hurlsgate were discharged on the evening of the 21st with the exception of the detachment of 20 men which were discharged on 22nd.

On the 22nd in the morning I proceeded to Wiscasset and there received information that the Enemy had been into the Damariscotta River and near to the fort which they did not choose to attack — being informed that there was ten Companies out for the defence of the town and various narrow passes in the River below Wiscasset. — An order for the discharge of all but three Companies was issued, the Magistrate of the place and some from other towns having requested this number of Companies for their defence, the officers who I assembled to side in with concuring with the Magistrate in opinion. — I did not think it my duty to discharge a larger number untill the pleasure of the Commander in Chief should be known, particularly after being informed of the situation of the garrison.

In order that I should be able to make up an opinion understandingly in relation to the number of Men that should be retained in service at and near Wiscasset, I sent for Capt. Perry the Commanding officer at the Fort and requested him to state to me what number of Men he considered necessary to defend his fort in case of attack. His answer one hundred at least. To the question how many men have you now in the fort —— he answered eight. — Capt Perry was informed that if he desired more Men and would make the request he should have them, his answer was, that he had no instructions to make any such request —— I consider it necessary to state these facts to show that we are not only not defended by the State but there is no disposition to do it. ——

From Wiscasset I proceeded on the 22nd to Damariscotta. Eight Companies from the Reg. of Col. Day had been out they were all discharged but one Company which was stationed at various places and will remain untill the pleasure of the Commander in

Chief is known. It may be considered as a fortunate circumstance that the Enemy did not attack the Fort at Damariscotta, as there was but one heavy gun and that without balls, they had taken the precaution to pick up stones to fire in case it was necessary to make defense.

The last information which I have had of the movement of the Enemy left them at St. Georges, were they had burnt some small vessels which is a subject of regret. The fort having one many only in it and the Militia not having been out in time has been destroyed, this while it encourages the enemy, will stimulate the Government of the States it is presumed to a little more exertion at least so far as respects their own fortifications —

I enclose a letter which I received from a gentleman taken on the 20th and who had an opportunity to obtain the most correct information which we have received. I enclose the copy of the Petition handed to me this morning from which I infer that there has been a larger number of Troops discharged than the safety of this plan will justify — it was quite an object with me to lessen the expense as much as possible in order to discharge the troops at Wiscasset, and Damariscotta. I considered it necessary first to discharge those who were ordered out here, as there had been one Company left in service in Damariscotta and three in Wiscasset. I am inclined to think I shall order out at least one Company at this place untill the pleasure of the Commander in Chief is known which I hope to be advised of by return of Mail as also his opinion in relation to the other companies now out.

The officers and soldiers have attended to the occasion of the present alarm with a promptness which does them honor, they have exercised the discretion on this occasion as directed by the Commander in Chief in a way that cannot I think fail to be satisfactory.

The officers having as they have done this independently in most of the cases after the necessary enquiry I have been so far satisfied as to approve their contact in every particular, and now only hope that the whole may be approved by the Commander in Chief.

> I am Sir respectfully
> *Your obt. Servant*

King evidently reserved this copy for himself, for there is no signature. It throws some light on his difficulties in directing the defense of the coast caused by the reluctance of the Massachusetts government to spend money to keep the militia on duty, for he was allowed to pay them only when called out on an alarm and to send all but a few home when it was over.

It is possible that Governor Strong was in no position at this time to help defend the District of Maine, whether he wanted to or not. Late in August, the British, in possession of all the Maine coast east of the Penobscot, began tightening their blockade along the entire east coast of the United States.

Boston commerce was at a standstill. Massachusetts ships were at anchor with inverted tar barrels or bags over their masts to prevent rotting, which were called "Madison's Nightcaps" by discouraged merchants. Traffic for trade was confined to "mud clippers," ox teams on muddy roads, or small boats hugging the coastline. Rebellious Federalists, unable to achieve an independent New England, were forced to defend themselves as best they could from British invasion.

The government at Washington, forced from its capitol, which was burned by invading British troops, could do little to help Governor Strong at this time. He called a special session of General Court and was to borrow money from the Massachusetts banks for defense. However, Senator Mark L. Hill reported to King that it was spent on the militia protecting Boston and surrounding towns. The District of Maine had second priority. This confirmed King's belief that the Federalists in the General Court would not raise an expedition to retake eastern Maine, nor would Governor Strong sponsor it.

In September, on an official tour to Camden, King learned that seven warships were sailing westward from Castine toward Lincoln County. He decided it was time to take further measures for defense. Alerting the militia along the way, he hastened back to Bath, and on September 10, 1814, ordered out the first brigade of his division. General McCobb and Colonel Reed at Phippsburg had already alerted their men when they received orders to have Colonel Reed's regiment ready to fortify Cox's Head. An earthworks was built up on the bald summit of the Head, where it commanded the entrance to the Kennebec River. All the materials used had to be taken up the hill from Colonel Reed's farm close by. This was hard work and some of the troops did not feel that this was what military service should be. The crude fort was armed with such cannon as they had at hand, including part of the armament of Popham Fort on Hunnewell's Point, and an old British gun now in Bath's Library Park. Colonel Reed's regiment remained at Cox's Head until October 1, and other units of the first brigade remained in Bath until the end of September.

Action in this war was very slow. Relying on the time it would take seven warships to sail westward to the Kennebec, King had time to mix pleasure with business when he inspected his coastal defense. Zina Hyde, major and the brigade executive, tells in his diary how they visited Cox's Head and Popham Fort to test their defenses under the date of Saturday, September 24, 1814:

> After breakfast, requested by Maj. J. F. Wingate (of Gen. King's staff) to attend Gen. King and others to the forts on Cox's head and on Hunniwell's Point. After consulting Gen. McCobb, set out from Gen. King's wharf with very pleasant weather. Our party consisted of Gen. King, Maj. Wingate, Mr. Greenwood (Andrew Greenwood Esq.), Maj. (Ebenezer) Clapp, Mr. C. Clapp, Mr. William K. Porter and myself. Stopped a short time to view the work on Cox's Head, where Col. Reed's regiment was on fatigue duty under Lieut. Eastman acting as engineer. Col. Reed had got one 24-pounder almost mounted. During our stop, sent the boat down to Capt. Wilson, commanding at the Point, to have him prepare a chowder for us. After a short stop at Cox's Head, proceeded to the Point where we partook of a very fine chowder. Inspected the works. Capt. Wilson fired a 12-pounder elevated to an angle of about four degrees, which sent a ball within a few feet of Pond Island, two miles distant, without striking. Gen. King also fired a 24-pounder, which did not carry so well, nor did he make so good a shot. Returned to Cox's Head. After spending a short time at the works and firing the first gun mounted for the first time, we embarked for Bath, sun about half an hour high, and arrived at eight o'clock.[8]

The British were taking their time. They were in no hurry to attack any particular place, secure in the knowledge that they had control of the coast and mostly interested in sending raiding parties ashore for fresh meat and vegetables when needed. On September 20, Major-General King had sent a dispatch to General McCobb to keep a lookout for British ships, for it was reported that the British squadron was off Boothbay at two that afternoon. The main part of the squadron continued out to sea, but H.M.S. *La Hogue* was off Seguin and hovered about for some time, for several brushes were had with barge parties from it visiting the Sheepscot. Colonel Reed sent two companies on scows across to Georgetown Island, over which they marched to the Sheepscot shore. They arrived just as the barges were returning and were set near the shore by a strong southeast wind. The militiamen promptly fired at them and the swivel guns aboard the barges fired in return. None of the militiamen were hit, but a musket ball shattered the musket in one man's hands. There were other skirmishes on the islands, and one British lieutenant was shot while he was pacing the deck of a barge as it sailed down the Sheepscot. The *La Hogue* did not stay, however. The British warships did not try to come up the Kennebec River, for passing the fort at the mouth of the river and the Cox's Head fortification would have been at the risk of damage to their ships. The earthen parapets of Popham Fort could stand a lot of pounding from their guns, while a well-placed shot from the land batteries could have seriously damaged their vessels.

The second mobilization at Bath was marked by an unfortunate incident. Major Benjamin Ames's squadron had been on patrol duty, so their inspection of arms had not been performed until the 13th of September. Their weapons had not been unloaded. Major Hyde was being assisted in the inspection by Nathan Ames, aide-de-camp on the brigade staff. The inspecting officers stood in front and a little to the left of the troop officers. Major Hyde examined each pistol with the muzzle carefully pointed to the ground, but Captain Nathan Ames pointed those he inspected upward. The inspection was almost over when one of the pistols went off in Captain Ames's hands and Lieutenant Baker, who was sitting on his horse just behind him, was instantly killed. The matter of the shooting was brought to a court investigation at General King's house, where it was decided that the act had been "carelessness."

Ames, some who did not like him said, put on an act of sorrow and was pardoned.

On December 22, 1914, Dearborn gave King orders to raise a force of 5,000 men to lead an expedition to retake Castine. Two days later, on December 24, a treaty of peace was signed at Ghent in which each party was to restore the territory conquered that belonged to the other, and provision was made for referring the ownership of the islands in Passamaquoddy Bay to a joint commission, as in the Treaty of 1783. News of the treaty traveled slowly and King was well along with his plans for an expedition when, on February 15, 1815, he received word that the war was over.

President Monroe appreciated King's efforts for defense, for when it came time for the British to surrender the territory formally, he wrote to Brigadier-General James Miller in the War Department as follows:

> As Major-Gen'l King was to have commanded the expedition against Castine, had it taken effect, it would, I have no doubt, be gratifying to him to be authorised to receive possession of it, according to the treaty, from the British Commander there. Should you have made no other arrangement, the President desires that you will commit this trust to him, and should you have appointed any other person, that you will associate him in it.[9]

James Miller, who forwarded this news to Bath, added that he had appointed Lt. Col. Starks and ordered him to proceed to Castine with a sufficient guard to take possession of the territory that had been occupied by the British forces in the District of Maine.

"Should King want to enter upon this service," he wrote, "the enclosed letter to Col. Starks will authorize him to associate with him and receive all necessary information in his possession."[10] There is no record in King's files that King took advantage of the invitation. Whether he did or not, no doubt he was pleased with the honor the President gave him for his attempts to defend the District. No one could appreciate more than King the joy and relief that the people felt when the British withdrew from their towns and they were free to go to sea again.

Governor Strong came to visit the Kings and commended William for his able leadership in the defense of the District, but probably the commendation King appreciated most came from a group of fellow citizens who met in a convention in 1816 and voted a resolution commending his efforts to protect the eastern section of the District of Maine from attack despite the negligence of and opposition by the government of Massachusetts to all military efforts on the part of the District to defend itself. The resolution was signed by Benjamin Ames, James McLellan, Joseph F. Wingate, Solomon Eaton, and John Coombs.

ABOVE The King mansion at Scarborough *Courtesy The Bath Marine Museum*

LEFT The Winter Street Church
Courtesy Charles E. Hewitt

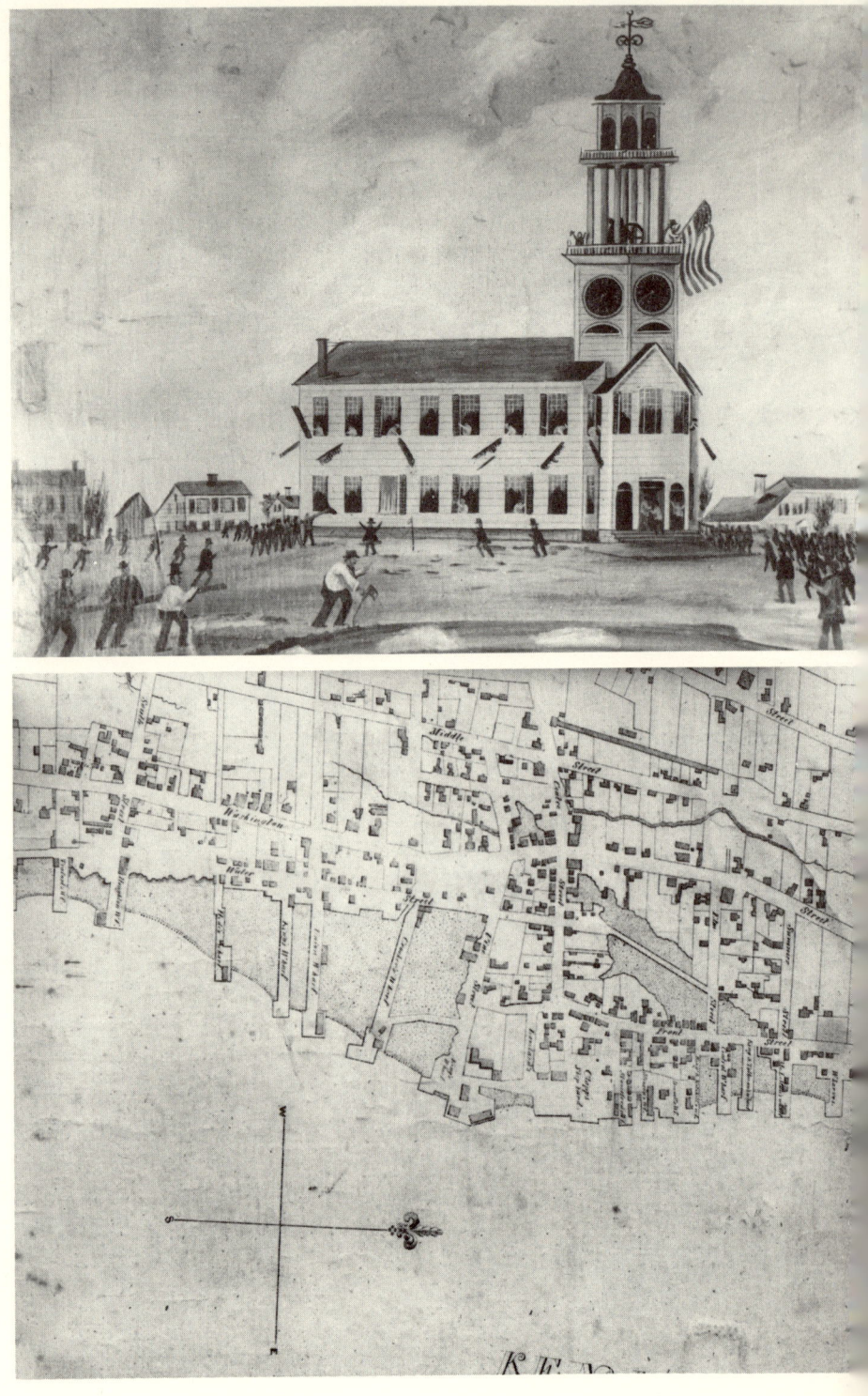

OPPOSITE PAGE TOP Destruction of the Old South Church *Courtesy The Bath Marine Museum*

OPPOSITE PAGE BOTTOM Map showing wharves along the Kennebec, several of which belonged to King or to King and one of his partners *Courtesy The Bath Marine Museum*

ABOVE Looking south on Front Street from the corner of Broad Street toward the First National Bank *Photo Courtesy Mary Baxter White.*

ABOVE A close-up of the eagle on the First National Bank *Courtesy The Bath Marine Museum*

BELOW Stonehouse Farm, where William King had his hunting lodge *Photo 1958 by B. Colby*

William King as a young man, painted c. 1806 by Gilbert Stuart *Courtesy The Bath Marine Museum*

Bath Dec 12, 1811

Capt David Foote
Sir the Brig Huron being now loaded with a cargo of lumber you will proceed the first favourable wind for the Island of Dominica, where you will dispose of your Cargo to the best advantage, you will by all means collect the amt you have formally left there even should you have to go to any other Island for a part of your payment but this you must avoid if possible.

You will take a clearance as from St Bartholomews and get a Certificate likewise of the Origin signed by two Merchants of that place purporting that it is the growth and produce of that Island.

This I presume you will be able to do without going down with your Vessel.

You will write frequently and give me particularly the State of your business.

Wishing you a fair wind and safe return I remain Respectfully Yours

Signed, William King

ABOVE Ann Frazier King, wife of William King, painted c. 1806 by Gilbert Stuart *Courtesy Maine State House Portrait Collection*

OPPOSITE PAGE TOP The Erudition School in Bath, erected in 1794 *Courtesy The Bath Marine Museum*

OPPOSITE PAGE BOTTOM Facsimile of a letter of instruction, 1811, to Captain David Foote from William King *Courtesy The Maine Historical Society*

ABOVE Painting by Francis Rittal, 1803, of the ship *Lady Washington Courtesy The Bath Marine Museum*

OPPOSITE PAGE The navigation book kept by Captain Francis Rittal, 1805 *Photo Abbie Sewall Schultz, Courtesy The Bath Marine Museum*

Francis Kittal's
Navigation book

May the Constitu[tion]
of
America bid defiance to all Europe[an]
Tyranny
August 17 1805

ABOVE Facsimile of a letter of instruction, 1812, to Captain Matthew Prior from William King
Courtesy The Maine Historical Society

RIGHT William King as an older man
Courtesy The Bath Marine Museum

TOP Governor King's house at Kingfield, Maine *Courtesy The Bath Marine Museum*

ABOVE This hotel served as a stagecoach terminal in Bath, but often the coach would pick up Governor King at his own house *Courtesy Charles E. Hewitt*

OPPOSITE PAGE TOP A typical vessel of the King period *Photo Abbie Sewall Schultz, Courtesy The Bath Marine Museum*

OPPOSITE PAGE BOTTOM Lithograph made from a sketch drawn by Cyrus W. King *Courtesy The Bath Marine Museum*

ABOVE RIGHT The William King Monument in Bath *Courtesy Diane Longley*

ABOVE LEFT Plaque on the King Monument *Courtesy Diane Longley*

TOP Elmwood House before it became the Shannon House and then was remodeled and became the King Tavern *Courtesy Charles E. Hewitt*

ABOVE This busy scene was taken soon after William King's home was moved to Vine Street and became a tavern *Courtesy The Bath Marine Museum*

TOP The Governor King Room in the Bath Marine Museum, showing his piano and bed *Courtesy The Bath Marine Museum*

ABOVE The King Tavern after its dormered roof had been removed to add a full fourth story *Courtesy The Bath Marine Museum*

LEFT Paneling of a second-story room in the King Tavern *Courtesy The Bath Marine Museum*

RIGHT The Franklin Simmons statue of Major General William King, in the Capitol Building in Washington, D.C. With Senator William S. Cohen (Republican, of Maine) are King family descendant Ludlow Elliman of Damariscotta and Mrs. Elliman *Photo Courtesy of Ludlow Elliman*

VII

THROUGHOUT the war, King and his business associates had carried on their banking and insurance businesses in Boston, Wiscasset, Bath, and Hallowell, though at a much slower pace. The Marine Insurance business in Boston, linked with their ships and shipping, was often called upon, as was the Boston Bank, to help in emergencies. This, added to his military duties, caused King to travel from Bath to Boston many times as well as to visit Portland on occasion. Doing business under Swedish and Spanish licenses brought risks to him and his agents, but under neutral colors, they stayed in business until strict enforcement of the blockade, when their vessels were tied up in various ports.

At the end of the war, however, the partners had business reverses, and King's business reached a low ebb. His vessels in the West Indies trade were bringing in some money, but were in need of repairs. His partner Dr. Porter, as treasurer of Bowdoin College, had financial difficulties. In the spring of 1814, a disastrous flood on the Androscoggin River at Brunswick and Topsham damaged twenty-one sawmills, a fulling mill, an aqueduct used in transporting lumber around the falls, a grist mill, and the cotton and woolen mills — all looms being destroyed. About $10,000 worth of Porter & King's logs were washed out to sea. A large amount of the property lost belonged to Dr. Porter, for whom King was the guarantor. When Porter's bonds as treasurer of Bowdoin College were defaulted, King had to pay them.

Benjamin Orr, a trustee of Bowdoin College, was responsible for attaching all of King's holdings in Bath to cover the loss of the college funds. This legal dragnet stopped all King's business activities, even his vessels ready to go to sea. King paid off the larger part of the debt to release his vessels, but he was bitterly angry with Orr, because he felt the act was a needless and malicious transaction; besides being a damage to his business, it was a direct impeachment of his integrity, and he told the trustees so in no uncertain terms. He suspected there was some political implication to the action, for Orr was a Federalist and he was a Republican. He blamed President Appleton of the college, too, and questioned his motives for visiting British-held Castine during the war.*

In return for King's help in his financial distress, Porter made out a bill of sale to King for the sum of $6,000 for three quarters of his ownership in the ship *Homer* and one for seven eighths of the ship *Typhys* for $6,000 more. In addition, to help the family, King took a mortgage on Porter's lovely home in Topsham and elected to pay the school expenses in Boston for his niece, Mary Porter.

He had other calls on his generosity about this time, too. Mrs. Knox, widow of General Henry Knox of Thomaston, and a friend of the family, asked him for money to pay for her son Harry's college expenses in Boston, using as security her property in Thomaston. King was agreeable and expended a considerable sum, but he balked at paying any more when he learned that Harry was squandering it on wine and women. When the loan came due, Mrs. Knox was unable to pay. She was finally persuaded to turn over some of her property — the wharf, store, and considerable farmlands — with the understanding that she could redeem them by paying back the loan. This brought no cash to King, for he had to have the property upgraded and pay the back taxes.

Deprived of further loans, Harry went to sea on a privateer, which was wrecked. He then tried to practice medicine, for which he was not qualified, and finally was put in jail for his debts. He

---

* King was reconciled to Bowdoin when President Allen took Appleton's place, and he acted as a trustee of that college from 1821 to 1849.

GENERAL WILLIAM KING

wrote a pitiful letter to King, begging him to pay his debts, so he could come home. Probably King did pay them, for Harry returned to Thomaston not long after. Later, Mrs. Knox was able to redeem part of her property and King acquired permanent ownership of the wharf, store, quarry, and part of the land. He lacked cash, however, when his brother-in-law in 1816 asked him for money to settle an estate, offering valuable land in exchange.

The winter of 1816-1817 was very severe. Many left Maine because of loss of crops and fear of starvation. There was much sickness, and among those ill with influenza was William King's mother. Mary was with the Porters in Topsham at the time, and although her sister came to help Betsy take care of her and Dr. Porter attended her, she died on May 28, 1816. Cyrus notified William, who was in Boston, and made arrangements for their mother's funeral and burial in the family cemetery in Scarborough, attending to all the details himself. Together they made plans for a monument.

The year 1817 brought more grief to William and Ann when he received a letter from his brother-in-law, Joseph Leland, with the news of the sudden death of Cyrus in Saco, on April 25, asking him and Ann to come to the funeral. This was an unexpected blow, for he had not known that his brother was ill. Cyrus had become a brilliant lawyer, of whom King was very proud, and he had already begun to champion William in the cause they shared for the separation of Maine from Massachusetts. After this, William offered Mary Caroline, Cyrus's oldest daughter, a home with him and assumed the responsibility for the education of the son, William Rufus. The other children stayed with their mother in Saco, where William often stopped on his way to and from Boston.

The Brunswick Cotton Factory had been badly damaged in the flood, and in June, King was called to Topsham to a meeting of the stockholders and found he would have to pay forty dollars for each share he owned in order to help pay the company's debts. His cash was so low that he had to sell some of his bank shares to pay for his factory shares. He tried to collect some of the money he had loaned, but found his debtors were as short of cash as he was. One man said he planned to sell his oxen to pay King but could not find a purchaser, and asked him to wait a while as he didn't want to butcher them for the money.

In 1817 King not only had financial trouble but political disappointment as well. He became a candidate for Lieutenant Governor with his friend General Henry Dearborn as candidate for Governor on the Republican ticket, but their party was defeated in favor of the Democrats.

That winter, hoping to improve navigation for his vessels on the river, King investigated the use of the steam engine. A letter from his nephew, James Gore King, third son of his brother Rufus of New York, probably explains why he decided against it.

New York
Feb. 4, 1817

William King Esq.

Dear Sir; In answer to your letter respecting a steam engine I have to inform you that Mr. McQueen, who is the manufacturer of steam engines in this city, & (a) man of very considerable intelligence & experience, gives me to understand that it would require for a boat of thirty tons burthen an engine of four or five horse power, and that it would cost, with an iron boiler, four thousand, and with a copper boiler, five thousand dollars, complete and set up for operation in the boat. You will observe that in fresh water (an) iron boiler would be sufficient, but in salt water, a copper boiler would be required. As to the draft of the boat, by increasing its beam, it need not draw more than fifteen inches of water.

If the distance on which this contemplated boat is to play be not over twenty-five miles, a horse boat would probably answer every purpose, not costing more than half as much as a steam boat, either for first cost or for annual support. Many reasons besides might be urged why a horseboat should be preferred to a steam boat at your place. In any event be pleased to command my services, either in further inquiries or ordering machinery to be made.

Present me & my wife kindly to Mrs. King and all friends with you, & believe me,

Yours truly,
James G. King[1]

Although King seemed to lose interest in steam engines for himself after this, the *Tom Thumb,* the first steamboat of its kind, was brought up the river and tied at his wharf in 1818. In 1822 Seward Porter built the first steamboat on the Kennebec and outfitted her at King's wharf. It was a scow called the *Kennebec*, equipped with a steam engine and paddle wheels, but the engine was too small and hardly able to stem the river current. Both the *Tom Thumb* and the *Kennebec* were used as excursion boats.

King had other things on his mind at this time. The weather had improved in the summer of 1817, and many people had returned to Maine, finding no better place to live. On September 28, Mary Elizabeth King, William and Ann's first child, was born, and her birth seemed to coincide with an increase of farming, lumbering, trading, and shipbuilding. King, happy with the birth of the baby and encouraged that he had survived the depression, became busy again with his trade and with making up for his losses. He had leased the Stonehouse Farm to Rufus Berry in March of that year for half the profits on crops and livestock. He was again interested in politics. In 1818 he was elected to the General Court.

Disgusted with the Federalists at Bowdoin College, whom he blamed for causing him financial loss over Porter's business, he helped sponsor the establishment of the Maine Literary & Theological Institution for Baptists. The General Court, largely Congregationalist, reluctantly granted the Baptists a township in the wilderness fifteen miles above Bangor, at that time not a good location for a school. It did not suit King, who was on the committee for the school, and as usual dominated it. With the help of some of the other members, he arranged to find a more suitable location, and Waterville was finally chosen. The Theological Department was opened in July 1818, and the Literary Department was opened in October 1819.

King's committee applied to the Massachusetts Legislature for $3000 for aid, the sum given Bowdoin College, but was turned down. The Legislature felt that the Baptists could supply their own aid if they wanted a school. The Baptists resorted to subscriptions and help from friends, and King did all he could to help them. However, the Theological Department was soon discontinued and the Literary Department became dominant. It was said that King recommended this, because he did not believe in religious creeds and dogmas. The subscriptions kept the institution alive until the state of Maine came to its rescue.*

King served as a trustee of the Institution from 1819 to 1848 when his health began to fail.

King wanted to keep his vessels at work and not expend more than absolutely necessary for repairs. He was impatient with those who questioned his judgment and irritated over his lack of cash when he received word that the *Typhys*, which he had acquired of Porter, was in serious need of repair. She had been doing well in trade with Liverpool and the southern states, but Captain Ezekiel Purington had discovered that her hull was rotten.

In December King's agent in Savannah notified him that it would cost $1,200 to repair the *Typhys* in order to bring her back to Bath. King replied that he would not consent to more than a slight repair and added that he was convinced that $100 was as much as need be spent to make her safe for a lumber voyage to the West Indies, which he thought better than to return to Bath in the winter months.

He went on to explain that there was always considerable decayed wood to be replaced and added that he feared Captain Purington's acquaintance with vessels was not such as to make him a competent judge in these cases. He thought the ship would be able to perform a West Indies voyage and only regretted that the old plank shers had already been removed. He ordered them to be replaced as cheaply as possible, for if she had to have any such repairs as Captain Purington stated, which he doubted, they would have to be removed again in order to effect them.

If the captain thought the West Indies would not be of any advantage, King wrote, he should get what freight he could for New York or Boston so as to meet expenses of the return trip if possible.

King had had a brig repaired in Baltimore, which he thought was not worth half the bill for repairs when completed, and he felt bitterly that he did not want another expense such as that. This time he was wrong, for he lost a good captain.

The agent, Mr. Batelle, let the captain read King's letter and the

---

*In 1821 the Institution was named Waterville College. It became Colby University in 1867, and Colby College in 1899.

GENERAL WILLIAM KING

captain quit the vessel, saying that if he had not the knowledge to know when a ship was unseaworthy, then he was not capable of sailing her or of disposing of her cargo, therefore he declined to take charge of her. The agent agreed with the captain. King had to have the *Typhys* stripped in Savannah. Some of her equipment was saved and the rest sold at auction. To take the place of the *Typhys*, King bought the *Ganges*, a slightly larger ship, and the *Asia*, built in Wiscasset. These were his last vessels.

VIII

WITH bitter thoughts of the way Massachusetts authorities had neglected to provide proper defense for the District of Maine in the war, and their lack of understanding of the government and business problems of the District, King decided to take up the fight again for separation from Massachusetts.

As early as January in 1785, a newspaper, the *Falmouth Gazette*, had been started to bring this issue before the people. Petitions to the Massachusetts government were considered treasonous at first, but as more and more demands were made between 1791 and 1797, the government was forced to consider the problem. Anti-separationists fought against the idea. They said the cost of the new government would be too much and that there were not enough men in the District qualified to run it. Above all, shipowners and seamen were opposed to separation for economic reasons. According to United States law then, every state was a district and only citizens of adjacent states were allowed to enter and clear their vessels without going through customs. New Hampshire separated Maine from Massachusetts, which meant that Maine vessels would have to go through customs formalities if Maine became a state, for Boston was Maine's most important port. At this time, merchants and shipowners depended entirely upon sails. Winds, tides, and weather conditions made departure delays for custom formalities a loss of money as well as time.

In 1807 William King and his separationist friends, during the winter session of the legislature, had urged the Democrat-Republican controlled General Court to allow Maine towns to vote on the question, because they felt Maine as a state would be better off. The people, however, elected a Democrat-Republican governor but rejected separation by a large margin. It was a severe blow to King and his friends' hopes; then the war intervened and no more action was taken.

Now friends were urging King to lead the fight again. Merchants found it hard to conduct their business because of taxes and Massachusetts regulation of trade; also there was added inconvenience and delay because important records were kept in Boston, the seat of government, which was too far away. This made law cases expensive. Outlying sections of the District were without representation in Massachusetts government and the people in those sections felt neglected.

In 1815 King had become the leader of a managing junto that included General Chandler, an old Democrat warhorse; John Holmes, clever lawyer, judge, and politician; William Pitt Preble, lawyer and shrewd political manager; and Judge Albion Parris, a commonsense, practical, hardworking politician. Senator King had intimate knowledge of the Massachusetts legislature and the ability to control a committee. They respected his judgment and listened to him. Two writers, Samuel Ayer and Samuel Whiting, joined the cause and spoke out for separation in the *Eastern Argus,* while writers in the *Portland Gazette* took up the cause of the anti-separationists.

On February 26, Senator Albion Parris introduced a resolution for separation, but the Senate turned it down. At this time, the balance of power had shifted to the Federalists, who feared that a new state with representatives and senators of the Republican party might form a majority in the United States Congress. The junto redoubled their efforts for separation, however, and obtained permission for a vote on the matter on May 20, 1816. This vote was a great disappointment to King and his friends, for only 17,000 of nearly 38,000 eligible voters went to the polls. Although there were more votes for separation than against it, not enough people had voted to assure Massachusetts authorities that Maine people wanted separation. Nevertheless the Maine congressmen petitioned for and were given terms of separation. A second referendum took place in September of 1816. The legislature directed the towns to choose delegates to meet in Brunswick the last day of September. If there was a vote of 5 to 4 in favor, the committee to form a constitution would be appointed. William King was chosen to be president of the convention and Samuel Whiting, secretary.

The vote count as turned in by the delegation was 11,969 yeas and 10,346 nays, far below the requirements, but the faction of Separationists was not prepared to give in easily. In fact, they had even discussed going so far as to lose nay votes. On a report drafted by the mathematician, William Pitt Preble, the committee to examine the returns contrived to show the majority of the towns in favor. This scheming was obvious and the legislature turned it down, declaring the convention had misconstrued the Act of Separation. The convention nonetheless appointed a committee to draw up a constitution and another to apply for statehood. Unfortunately for them, the General Court dissolved the convention before they could accomplish their task.

Although King listened with sympathy to the various plans, he was not blamed for the unethical behavior of his colleagues. The worst that could be said of him was that his appointments had weighed the election returns in favor of the Separationists.

It was obvious that new tactics would have to be employed, but for a time after the defeat of the Act of Separation, the men of the junto went their separate ways. William, keeping one hand on his business, however, was determined to keep in touch with his group and party. He ran for senator of Lincoln County in 1818 and was elected. He found the Federalists strong in Massachusetts and the District of Maine's representatives playing only minor roles in the affairs of state. Under these conditions, King felt the junto would have to plan carefully and work harder to separate Maine from Massachusetts. This time there must be no mistakes or bungling strategy.

After some meetings with the junto and much correspondence with friends, King began working to elect men to the General Court who were in favor of separation. Believing that the customs law was one of the most important obstacles to separation, he asked the Maine members of Congress to bring up a revision of the law, but it was defeated. He then decided to go to Washington himself and see what he could accomplish. First he consulted his brother Rufus, who was a recognized authority on commercial matters in the United States Congress. Rufus promised he would do all he could to have the law revised. Next he talked to Secretary of the Treasury William H. Crawford, who had charge of administering and regulating the coastal trade laws. Crawford could see the need for the change. He and King agreed politically and he wanted King's backing for him to succeed Monroe as President, so he promised to do what he could to have the law revised. Reassured that there was a good chance of a revision of the coastal trading laws, King returned to the Massachusetts General Court.

There he learned that interest in separation was mounting in Maine, but he did not feel that the time was right to bring up the subject in the Court. More work must be done in the District to stir up the interest of the people, and he wanted the coastal bill passed before proposing separation again. A number of facts seemed to favor his party. Many Baptists in the district were unhappy over the lack of support given them by the Federalists in the General Court for their college in Waterville. Methodists, increasing in numbers in Maine, felt the Federalists discriminated against them, too. By 1819 the Baptists and Methodists who favored King's party outnumbered the Federalists in voting power.

King and his friends were taking no chances. They increased their pleas for voters to come to the polls and vote for separation. The *Argus* printed their views. Broadsides were printed, stating that as a state the district would be able to govern itself more cheaply than under Massachusetts. Their taxes would be spent in the state, rather than go to Boston, and nonresident taxes would be adjusted to benefit residents instead of "foreigners." All in all, sentiment was swinging toward approaching separation, but King was waiting until he received the news that the customs revision had been passed.

When the welcome news arrived, the *Argus* headlined it, and explained how the new law did away with the division of the coast along state boundaries; intead, the Atlantic and Gulf coastline was divided into two districts, one running from Eastport in Maine to the Perdido River in Florida and the other from Florida to the Louisiana-Texas boundary. Moses Carleton of Wiscasset and David Payson, who had led the last anti-separationist movement, now joined King and publicly sponsored separation. Only the diehards were left.

In May 1819, when the new legislature in Massachusetts convened, seventy towns from the District of Maine petitioned for separation, and a bill in favor of it passed the two houses. It became a law on the 19th of June 1819. On the fourth Monday of July, the people of the District of Maine voted 17,091 for and only 7,132 against separation. The Governor of Massachusetts issued a proclamation announcing the results on August 24.

On October 11, 269 delegates from the towns assembled at the courthouse in Portland to organize the new government. William King was again chosen president of the convention and Robert C. Vose was chosen secretary. A committee of thirty-three members was formed to draw up the constitution. Party feeling was good, and King, who had promised to be fair in giving out offices, chose the men he thought best qualified — regardless of party.

A special committee of nine members was chosen to submit a name for the new state. Their first choice was "Commonwealth of Maine," and the debate that followed brought out some interesting points of view. Mr. Parsons, of Edgecomb, moved to strike out "Commonwealth" and insert "State," to save time and expense of writing and printing. Judge Thatcher supported him, saying it would be easier than writing "Commonwealth." Mr. Cutler, of Farmington, explained they were in a measure attached to it; Mr. Preble thought it more respectable, while Judge Daniel Cony was in favor of it as a privilege carried over from the Commonwealth of Massachusetts. The more practical overruled, however, and "Commonwealth" was replaced by "State," 119 to 113. Then someone moved to strike out "Maine" and insert "Columbus" for the name of the state. Mr. Vance spoke against this move, saying that Maine "is the name by which we are known in this country and in Europe. All our maps, our plans and records, have that name as the designation of the Territory. If it were altered, perhaps half a century would pass away before the new name were as well known."[1]

Judge Cony urged that they consider the name Columbus, for he thought the new community should be consecrated "by performing a long-delayed act of justice, and calling it Columbus." He thought "Columbus had been cheated of his rightful glory of giving his name to the continent, and that Maine suggested nothing great or distinguished. . . .

"Judge Thatcher replied that he did not wish to deprive old Columbus of any of his honors, but he 'did not discover this part of the continent, nor did he know, as long as he lived, that the continent he discovered extended to these latitudes' . . . He thought the name Columbus . . . 'would more naturally carry the mind to some part of South America. . . . The District of Maine is everywhere known as to its situation, commerce and products.' The convention was wisely of the same mind, and the motion to strike out 'Maine' was lost."[2] The vote was 140 to 101, and King and other businessmen were relieved.

Meanwhile, the constitutional drafting committee used the Massachusetts constitution as a pattern, though they changed voter requirements, representation, and assessment of real estate. A council replaced the lieutenant governor. Freedom of speech, press, and religion was assured.

William King and some of his Republican friends were especially interested in Article VIII of the constitution, entitled Literature. King, with the education of Maine people in mind, had previously discussed this subject with Thomas Jefferson, whose opinion he valued highly. They had agreed that in a democracy it was necessary that the general public be educated. Massachusetts had provided for education and the committee believed that Maine should do the same. The Legislature was authorized to see that Maine towns made suitable provisions at their own expense to support and maintain public schools and endow colleges, academies, and seminaries when needed.

The matter of colleges, however, took much of the committee's time and thought — Bowdoin College, especially. The

Congregationalist founders of Bowdoin, mostly Federalists, did not favor religious freedom at the college or the democratic principles of the Republican Party. King felt that Bowdoin should be free of religious restrictions. Massachusetts Federalists, wishing to protect the college from "illiterate Democrat-Republicans," had written into their charter that the President, Trustees and Overseers of the college would hold and enjoy their powers and privileges in all respects. They were not to be altered, annulled or restrained except by judicial process of the law — safe from the Republicans, they thought. Judah Dana, a lawyer from Fryburg whom King consulted, believed with King that colleges should not be the home of religious privilege. He advised King to wait until, as they expected, King would be governor. He pointed out a loophole in the Articles of Separation by which the Legislature could increase the number of trustees and overseers, allowing more Republicans than Federalists to be nominated. President Appleton was very ill and soon would have to be replaced, and it was suggested that Democrat William Allen would be a good candidate. Also Article VIII contained the provision that "no donation, grant or endowment shall at any time be made by the legislature to any literary institution now established, or which may hereafter be established, unless, at the time of making such endowment, the legislature of the state shall have the right to grant any further powers to alter, limit or restrain any of the powers vested in, any such literary institution, as shall be judged necessary to promote best interests thereof."

Lured by the prospects of the Legislature to establish a state medical school, William Allen, who was accepted as president of Bowdoin after Appleton died on November 13, 1819, persuaded the governing board to submit to state control, paving the way for the governor, with the approval of the Legislature, to increase the number of overseers and trustees of the college and free it of Federalist control.

Before all this could take place, however, Maine had to become a state. On December 8, 1819, the Maine Statehood Bill was submitted simultaneously to both the House and Senate, but an unexpected obstacle threatened to prevent its passage for some time. The obstacle was slavery, not in Maine, but in Missouri, also seeking statehood. The Senate, wishing to retain its balance between slave and free states, added to the Maine bill an amendment enabling Missouri to establish a constitution without restriction to slavery. Maine idealists, angered by this unwarranted connection, fought against it or any other compromise that would implicate Maine with the cause of slavery. King's mail was full of letters from representatives in Washington seeking advice on what to do. King did not favor slavery, but he was worried that Maine would lose her chance to become a state. He knew he had his brother Rufus's help. The pressure on the delegates was increased by the fact that Maine would revert to Massachusetts control if her bid for statehood was not accepted by March 4, 1820. King's friend Mark Langdon Hill was also working hard to accomplish it.

Just when it seemed that Maine would be sacrificed, a Senate and House Committee effected the famous Missouri Compromise, permitting Maine to become a free state and Missouri a slave state for the concession that no territory above 36° 30" parallel could enter the Union as a slave state. Maine was freed of Missouri and entered the Union as the twenty-third state on her own merit. The vote came on the third of March, just one day before Massachusetts General Court would have taken control of the District again.

IX

DURING these years of tension, while William was in Boston on business or traveling to Portland or Washington on matters of state, Ann, unable to accompany him, remained at home on Front Street in Bath. At times she was never quite sure where she could reach him to tell him news of home and their little daughter. After Christmas Day 1818, she wrote:

> You observe you have received my letter dated on Christmas Day. I previously wrote you a long letter and directed it to New Youk (York?) to the care of C. King presuming you would see him on your return. in it I gave you all the particulars respecting our little daughter. Since you left she has enjoyed perfect health. The last week she weigd a little over 28 pounds. She does not articulate more words than when you left but she makes sounds that we perfectly understand, she takes us by the hand and leads us to what she wants frequently to the kitchen and points to the dresser for her milk. She is entirely weaned from her bottle, takes nothing during the night, and I do not keep the lamp burning but she will not suffer me to turn my face from her. She awakes me every morning by saying papa all gone and then pretends to cry — she is good when we give her all our attention — she has grown pretty, has a great deal of colour and her hair curls — She has worn out three pairs of shoes since you left and now stamps about

with leather ones — She is geting to be afraid of strangers — will hide her face in my lap if anyone knocks at the door. I shall try to prevent it if possible as it will make her troublesome. She has not been out of the house since you left. My reason for keeping her so close is in concern of the hooping cough preveling around us — Mrs. Richardson's children have had it all winter.

Last week, Mr. Littlefield was repairing the sink. She was playing with the shavings and threw them in my face. Some lint lodged in my Eye which made me blind for a week it had to be removed by washing with a brush which was extreamly painful however the inflamation is gone of and the sight is nearly as strong as ever — You will receive this on Friday morning. I hope you will write the same day that I may hear on Sunday. Do remember that all the pleasure I can have while you are absent is in hearing from you —

> Yours with the truest affection
> Ann M. King[1]

On December 28, 1818, Ann wrote another letter direct to Boston:

Dear Husband,
Col. Wingate has just left me, I must confess I could hardly command my feelings sufficiently to welcome him so great was my disappointment at not seeing you, I had heard that he was in Boston and did not for an instant doubt that you was with him. You therefore can conceive of my feelings when I heard he had arrived without you.

Your letters during your absence have afforded me much pleasure. They have assured me of your health and happiness, and I feel proud when contemplating the figure you make among our greatest men. This long seperation is truly painful but when I consider the advantages that may occur in consequence of it I endeavor to be reconciled.

You complain of my not writing, but you have not particularly requested it and our friends have repeitedly told me that a letter could not reach you at Washington, therefore I have denied myself the pleasure of writing.

Nothing of consequence has developed since you left the same dull rotation business goes on as usual. Our little Darling has continued well since you left. About ten days since she weighed twenty eight pounds, She does not speak more words, than when you left, but she makes herself understood by signs. She will lead us to the kitchen, and when hungry to the closit for Cake, in the morning she wakes very pleasantly her first voice is papa all gone and then makes believe cry. . . .

General Wingate leaves for Boston in a few days. I wish I could go with them. I think I could go with them but must wait till you request it, if you conclude to send for us you must make all my arrangements, what I am to do with the House who is to drive me likewise my dear Husband you must consider that I cannot go from home without being at considerable expense as it is six years since I have appeared in the fashionable world.

I cannot but hope . . . . you will write me often. tell me exactly what your wishes are, and I hope I shall in every respect conform to them —

Col Wingate recomends my directing to the care of Charles King New York.

> Your truly affectionate
> *Ann M. King*[2]

The next letter Ann wrote to William explains why she did not go to Boston and how she felt about her husband's long absence.

> January 19, 1819

Yours, my Dear Husband informing me of your arrival at Boston of this day received. It gave me plesure as far as it assured me of your safety, but to hear that you was not to return to your family after an absence of nearly two months is indeed painful, but reasons you give for staying from me I dare say are good, but still I am not reconciled to them, in all your letters of late you have mentioned seeing me soon. Of course I expected you would return, but my life for some years past has been repleat with disappointments and I sometimes fear that I have already received my portion of happiness. — You mention something about my going to Boston to return with you. I presume you are not in ernest or you would have made some arrangements for me to go on, and directed me how to dispose of my family. John, you recolect has never drove of course I could not take him, but that is but of little consequence, the reasons you gave me before you left why I could not go to Boston are sufficient, and as I am convinced that I could not be their without puting you to much expence exclusive of board and traveling, I have determined on staying at home. you certainly will approve my determination when you consider my motive...[3]

Busy with his work in the legislature and plans for bringing about the separation of the District of Maine from Massachusetts, in addition to tending his shipping interests in Boston and the numerous calls he had from friends and relations to find positions or promotions in government and militia, William did not fully realize or appreciate Ann's feelings over his long absences from home. Soon after he received her January letter, however, he left Boston for the long ride home. He had much to think about. He would have to stop in Saco to take care of some of his brother's debts and visit the family, also to make arrangements to pay his nephew's school expenses. His brother-in-law, his sister Paulina's husband, was angry over the sales he had made of some Porter property, which he would have to explain. His ships were doing well in the West Indies. At St. Lucia, Captain Haddean reported good sales in boards, staves, oars, and masts. There was also a need for cattle, horses, fish oil, molasses, and rum for freight. Captain McKown, however, had reported his vessel leaking, saying they were losing their drinking water due to the oakum working out of the seams. The vessel would have to be tied up for repairs. In Boston his agents were chartering freights for his ship the *Volant* and the brigs *Huron, Eleanor,* and *Henry.* The *Homer,* a slow sailer, was in need of repair and would have to be sold. He needed to adjust the insurance on his ship *Asia,* which he had recently bought. Perhaps he could take Ann on a ride to Wiscasset and Thomaston while he settled his insurance and his business over the Knox property, or maybe she might want to go to Topsham to visit Betsy while he made arrangements to sell the Porter's mill shares. All these matters and more must have occupied his thoughts as he neared home to receive Ann and his little daughter Mary Elizabeth's welcome.

On Christmas Day, 1819, Ann was again unhappy, for William was away when their son Cyrus William was born. She wanted her husband to share the joy of the children they had waited so long to have. A letter found among his business letters shows how she felt:

... Nothing has prevented my writing before my beloved husband but the excessive weakness in my eyes — I avail myself of the first permission from Dr. B. to inform you that I am quite recovered. Our little son is doing well now but has been much troubled with a sore mouth, he has added a pound to his weight notwithstanding, and is newly a most beautiful child every one allows. Mary Elizabeth's face is nearlly well. She has become a good girl and very fond of her brother, she is going up stairs and down continually — Dr. Bartelett has called to see me and reported abroad that my Boy is by far the *handsomest* of the little strangers.[4]

On January 17, Ann wrote again telling William her health was recovering, but that she was tired with the care of the baby. Her servant "Catty" had returned to help her. The baby was better and Mary Elizabeth was walking up and down stairs and saying, "Tell papa to bring some plums and I will give some to my baby brother." Ann wished for his return to see the children. She had heard that the ship *Reunion* was lost and hoped the crew was saved and that it was insured.* She was pleased with Mrs. Wingate's friendship and Mark Hill's letter of congratulation on the birth of their son.

Soon after he received this letter, William returned to Maine for a purpose close to his heart. He had taken time in 1804 to become a charter member and first master of the Solar Lodge of Masons in Bath, according to Ralph J. Pollard, Grand Lodge historian, and had since been as deeply concerned with the formation of a Grand Lodge of Masons for Maine, as he was with the separation of the District of Maine from Massachusetts. He had served as one of the successful petitioners to the Grand Lodge of Massachusetts for the formation of a Maine Lodge; and when the meeting for its organization was held, though he could not be present, he was unanimously selected as the first Grand Master of the new lodge. A committee was sent to notify him. He accepted the office and agreed to be present at an adjourned meeting the following night for installation. According to an article in the *Eastern Argus* of January 27, 1820, describing the proceedings, King kept his word:

On Saturday last the Lodge of Free and Accepted Masons of Maine was consecrated in this town (Portland) . . . At Rev. Payson's Meeting House the exercises, consecration and installations took place, then they returned to Mason's Hall and partook of a rich repast. The first toast was by the Grand Master, William King, and was, "To the memory of our Grand Master, the illustrious Washington."

Some of the officers installed with King that day were Simon Greenleaf, Deputy Grand Master; William Swan, Senior Grand Warden; Nathaniel Coffin Jr., Grand Warden, and Elijah Kellogg, first Chaplain. Coffin was a nephew-in-law of King, having married his sister Paulina's daughter, Mary Porter.

X

IN 1820, King, at the height of his power, became governor of the State of Maine. As governor, it is doubtful that he had much time to spend with Ann and the children, though he was more often home in the spring of 1820. In January, William Preble had called for William King's nomination for governor, also that he be acting governor until the elections in April. He was absorbed in the launching of a new state into the Union and seeing that it would function properly. He had little time for his home. The *Eastern Argus* of Portland, Tuesday, March 21, 1820, describes the celebration that took place in Union Hall in that city on March 16.

> Thursday last witnessed the birth of a new State, and ushered *Maine* into the Union. That day was noticed, as far as we have heard from various towns, by every demonstration of joy and heartfelt congratulation, becoming the occasion. In this town salutes were fired in the morning, at noon, and at sunset, — the independent companies were under arms, and appeared in their usual style of military excellence, — the ships in our harbor displayed their flags — the Observatory and adjacent buildings were brilliantly illuminated, in the evening, and the celebration closed with a splendid ball. . . .
>
> May the day, which has so auspiciously commenced our political existence as a State, long be remembered with complacent

feelings and every annual return bring with it, by the many blessings it may produe, additional inducement for its celebration.

King was in Portland that day and attended the ball for a short time in the evening. On his return to Brunswick a few days later, he was met by a group of mounted military officers and a detachment of cavalry, who escorted him to his seat in Bath.

Ann was proud of the part William had in the making of a new state and the reception he received on arriving home, but she knew there was much more work to come. He would have to settle down in his office to read his mail filled with petitions for positions in the new government. Much would depend on wise decisions. He would probably make some enemies, but the state's welfare would come first. Ann resigned herself to attending household affairs and keeping the children from disturbing him, thankful to have him home and to have guests to break the monotony.

On the first Monday in April 1820, elections were held and King was elected governor almost without opposition, 21,083 votes in a total of 22,014. The Legislature was elected at the same time and met in Portland on the thirty-first of May.

Governor King in his first message to the people paid a generous tribute to Massachusetts. He said, "The political connection which has so long subsisted between Massachusetts and Maine being dissolved, it is a source of much satisfaction to reflect, that the measures adopted for its accomplishment, have effected the object in the most friendly manner. . . ." Then King went on to say that though a large majority of the Legislature which passed the Act of Separation was from Massachusetts proper, and therefore could make what demands they pleased, "the principles on which they acted were so equitable and just as to receive the general approbation. By this correct and wise course of policy the executive and legislative departments of that government have laid the foundations of a lasting harmony between the two States. . . ."[4]

While campaigning, King had proposed that if the Federalists of Maine would come into the effort of separation and use their influence with the Federalists of Massachusetts to accomplish it, the political patronage of the new state would be fairly and honorably divided between the parties in proportion to two Republicans to one

Federalist. Mr. William Drew in a later summary, which appeared in the *Lewiston Journal* of April 17, 1875, and was quoted in the *Bath Daily Times,* May 14, 1875, describes King's method of carrying out his promises:

> An organized and persistent effort was made upon him by his party friends to ignore the arrangement, and now he was in power to confine his appointments to them, but like a pillar of iron he stood erect and stiff to his purpose. Carefully and faithfully he distributed all the offices within the gift of the executive one-third to the federalists and two-thirds to republicans, seeking to equalize the same, by giving the most important ones to the former. Hence, in organizing the Supreme Court he appointed Prentiss Mellen (a federalist) Chief Justice, and Wm. P. Preble and Nathan Weston (republican) Associate Justices. So in organizing the State Court of Common Pleas, he made Ezekiel Whitman (federalist) Chief Justice of that, and Perham Smith (republican) Associte. Thus he went through the State in appointment of Sheriffs, Clerks of Court, Judges and Registers of Probate, Attorney Generals, Adjutant Generals, County Attorney, etc., etc.

The Senate elected John Chandler president. Being chosen shortly afterward a senator in Congress, he was succeeded in the chair by William Moody, a senator from York County; Moody was, however, in a few days, appointed sheriff of his county, when William D. Williamson succeeded him. Benjamin Ames was chosen speaker of the House of Representatives. On the Council were Thomas Fillebrown, William Webber, Mark Harris, Abiel Wood, William C. Whitney, Isaac Lane, and William Emerson. Ashur Ware was chosen secretary of state; and Joseph C. Boyd, treasurer. John Holmes, of Alfred, and John Chandler, of Monmouth, were elected senators to represent the new state in the United States Congress. Erastus Foote was made attorney general and Simon Greenleaf, reporter of decisions.

Among the senators in the new Maine Legislature were a number who had served in the Massachusetts Senate and knew the procedure. The judiciary code of laws was revised. More money was appropriated for the common schools.

On the joint commission of the two states prescribed by the Act of Separation, Massachusetts appointed Timothy Bigelow and Levi Lincoln. Maine appointed Benjamin Jones Porter and James Bridge. These four chose Silas Holman and Lathrop Lewis to complete the commission.

One of the first duties of the Legislature was to agree upon the Great Seal of the State. Judge Cony sent King a description of the seal and asked Ann's opinion for the color of the background from samples enclosed.

William F. Drew, in his article in the *Lewiston Journal,* gave King's views and attitude on the office of lieutenant governor and the Maine Council, as well as the part King believed Maine people should play in their government:

> There are one or two facts in relation to Gov. King, which it may not be out of place here for me to name. Conversing with him one day a few years after his retirement from all his public duties, the writer was expressing to him the improvement in the Maine constitution over that of the parent State, in dispensing the useless office of Lt. Governor. With some spirit he replied that he "did not think it an improvement, or a useless office. There should be a Lt. Governor," said he, "not only one of the people's choice to take the place of a vacating governor, but to preside at the council board and give the casting vote when necessary. When I was governor," continued he, "I laid my nominations before the council, *never allowed myself to be present when they were acted upon,* lest my presence should embarrass their free and independent action as to their confirmation. Hence, it was my practice, in certain cases, to make Lt. Governor of the senior councellor, and call him to the chair as presiding officer. Respect to the board and its action required this, as I considered."
>
> Sitting by the side of the ex governor in one of the seats near the Speaker's desk when the House of Representatives was in session, I remarked, in casting an eye over the chamber, that the seats appeared nearly all to be occupied by new members, which I thought was an unfortunate provision in the constitution, which districted towns for the election of representatives, whereby old and experienced legislators were necessarily excluded to make room for novitiates in the business. He did not agree with me. He thought that the system was a wise one, inasmuch as it brought

regularly a greater number of citizens into the legislature to become acquainted with the business of the State, whereby each one acquired a good amount of knowledge to carry home with him and spread amongst the inhabitants. The idea seemed a considerate one, and I could respectfully defer to it.

It seems that the lessons King learned from Thomas Jefferson had been learned well.

Although the state's first capitol was in Portland until a permanent location could be decided upon, when there were special guests, Ann acted as official hostess for the new state in their lovely home on Front Street in Bath. King's friends liked the little lady and often asked to be remembered to her in their letters to him.

Mrs. Joshua Wingate, who lived on top of the hill on Washington Street, also entertained a great deal. Though their husbands were of different political parties, the ladies were very good friends. According to a story from Henry Owen's *History of Bath,* an event of more than local importance took place there in September of King's first year as governor. It brought out how seriously men took their political views. King had hoped by fair measures to bring more harmony to his government, and Ann and Mrs. Wingate hoped through social affairs to bring a better feeling between the members of the two political parties.

Mr. Owen writes:

> A social event of September, 1820, which was of more than local importance at the time, and a really notable occasion, was the marriage of Charles Z. Clapp of Portland and Miss Julia Octavia Wingate of Bath at the house . . . at the top of Washington Street hill. The bride of that day was the daughter of Gen. Joshua Wingate, Jr., who was one of the cultured and wealthy men of the town and who had filled with credit the difficult post of collector of customs throughout the troublesome period of the embargo and the war of 1812, and she was a granddaughter of Gen. Henry Dearborn of Gardiner who was a military officer of distinction and President Jefferson's secretary of war. The bridegroom was one of the prominent men of Portland. As might be expected, there were many important people of the time among the guests, including Governor King, Gen. Dearborn, Commodore Jesse D.

Elliot and Gen. Simon Bernard who had served on Napoleon's staff at Waterloo.

Mrs. Wingate was one of the most beautiful women Maine ever produced, and was a famous hostess. Her husband also was generous and hospitable, and their house was the scene of many entertainments. There is an anecdote concerning them, illustrative of the time, which is worthy of repetition. Bath at this period, like most Maine communities, was rent with political animosities. People took their politics most seriously, so much so that Democrats (Republicans) and Federalists were often not on speaking terms. Churches and families were sometimes disrupted by politics. Bitterness was at its height when the General and his lady issued invitations to a party to celebrate the opening of their house, taking no account of political boundaries. As both host and hostess were highly and generally esteemed and their hospitality famous, the response was equally general. The spacious drawing rooms were filled, but Mrs. Wingate was overwhelmed with anxiety and despair when she perceived that her guests were eyeing one another askance. Not only did conversation languish, but coolness and restraint were everywhere in evidence amongst the company. What could she do? Suddenly she had a happy thought.

"Wingate," said the lady to her lord whom she always addressed by his surname, "Send for Terpsichore! Let us have music and dancing." It was done, the music struck up, and the guests were soon in graceful motion, and though throughout the evening the words spoken were brief and few, the evening was saved, and Federalists and Democrats long afterward talked of the happy occasion.[2]

King's election to the position of governor in April 1820 had been for the remainder of the year, but he accepted a renomination from the Democrat members of the Legislature and was elected without serious opposition for another year in 1821. As he rode over the rough roads from his home in Bath to Portland or took the steamboat, he had much time to think deeply about the state institutions and government appointments. His mail was filled with appeals for appointments and advice for offices. His thoughts seemed to anticipate the days of civil service reform in his message to the Legislature for 1821:

> The people of Maine have had too much reason to deplore the violence of a party administration which for a series of *years* selected all its officers from a minority. This mode of disposing of the public employments exclusively with a view to party, has fortunately at the present day but few advocates. Nor have I thought it would be consistent with the harmony that so happily prevails, or just in itself to confine the selection exclusively to those of a more particular sect or party. I ask, therefore, a continuance of the candor and liberality of my fellow-citizens while engaged in correcting these errors — a task which I assure them shall not be entailed upon my successor.[3]

King, however, was to find that human nature being what it is, harmony was not to prevail.

William D. Williamson, who was an associate with King in the founding of the state, says in his *History of Maine*, "It may be worthy of remark, that during the primary political year, a period of 17 months, all the constitutional provisions for filling the Executive chair, were called for and improved."[4]

Governor King that next year recommended measures encouraging the development of manufacturing industries in the state. His own business had given him an understanding of Maine's possibilities and he hoped to begin industry that would put the state on a firm business foundation. His experience with the cotton factory in Topsham and its struggle for existence caused him to initiate a proposal to tax manufacturers at a nominal rate for a period of time in order to induce them to come to Maine and survive, but the democratic farmers in the Legislature felt that this would give the businessmen an unfair advantage and they turned it down.

King was interested in farming as well as manufacturing. He grew apples and potatoes as well as other crops on his farm for his coastal and West Indies trade. As a member of the Maine Agricultural Society he was interested in improving crops and livestock as well as in the care and preservation of Maine's timberlands. He had dreams of establishing a progressive farming and lumbering town in his Bingham Purchase in Kingfield and had already laid the foundation for what he hoped would be a thriving community.

He was disappointed by the defeat of another of his plans for Maine. He wanted the state to control all of the public lands within her borders. He induced the Legislature to appoint a committee to negotiate with the Massachusetts Commissioner for the purchase of Massachusetts's share of Maine wildlands. The commissioners came to an agreement, but both legislatures turned it down.

XI

ALTHOUGH King was busy launching a new state into the Union, he kept in touch with his friends, captains, and agents outside the state, and with what was happening there. Much of his business at this time was in the southern states and the West Indies.

Spanish government had not improved along the Florida coast. At the time of the Louisiana Purchase, Spain had declared east and west Florida not a part of the purchase. West Florida included at that time Alabama and Mississippi, where United States citizens had settled and were unhappy with Spanish authority. During the War of 1812, the Spanish had allowed the British to use Pensacola Harbor for their ships. General Andrew Jackson had retaliated by invading Spanish territory and taking over the city. East Florida had become a refuge for runaway slaves and pirates. King and his friends had lost ships and cargoes in the waters off Florida and no amount of protest was recognized by Spanish authorities. United States Navy vessels had to be ordered into the area to protect shipping.

The Creek and Seminole Indians, living in peace with the Spanish, often made raids into the southern states. In 1817 the Seminoles started a small-scale war in Georgia. President Monroe demanded that Spain restore order and sent Andrew Jackson into Georgia to stop the Indians. Jackson overstepped his authority, invaded Florida, took two Florida forts, burned Indian towns and executed two Englishmen who, he said, were inciting the Seminoles to invade the United States. Spain protested and Monroe ordered the troops withdrawn. Disgusted, John Quincy Adams, Secretary of State, told Spanish officials that if they could not keep order they should get out of Florida.

Not long after this, to the surprise of the United States officials, Spain offered to give up all of Florida and nearby islands, as well as her claims in Oregon, if the United States would pay the $5,000,000 damage claims individual Americans had against her. Early in December 1820, King received letters from Mark L. Hill, John Chandler, John Holmes, and others about the impending treaty. When it was ratified they said there would be need of commissioners to pay off the claims. They wanted him to come to Washington to represent the New England mechants, and they were consulting the President as to King's appointment.

King was busy with the business of the new State of Maine, but he gave them assurance that he might be interested if they really needed him and the President was agreeable. His friends, anxious for his help, kept him in constant touch with their progress. Chandler finally reported in a letter dated February 19, 1821, that "this day the Spanish Treaty was ratified." He added that he was glad King was recovering from an indisposition (which was something rare, for King was seldom sick), and if Mrs. King was with him, he would thank him to make his respects to her.

King, convalescing, had had time to think. He had helped in the separation of Maine from Massachusetts, and established the state on a firm foundation. There were capable men in office who could carry on his work. He was a businessman, deeply interested in the shipping trade. Merchants who had lost much during the Spanish control in the Carribbean trade were anxious for his help. They said they wanted a strong man in Washington to represent them; in addition, if he were there he might promote the interest of his friend William H. Crawford for President in the coming election.

King was soon recovered and back in Portland. He needed to continue the state's business while awaiting a decision from Washington. Among other actions, he sent his brother-in-law Dr. Benjamin Porter, to investigate possible illegal cutting of timber along the state's northern border, and made arrangements for a lighthouse on Cross Island and a marine hospital in Bath. He made more appointments and discussed them with his council. Complaints over tax payments were adjusted.

In preparation for leaving for Washington, King's own business took some of his time. The lime business in Thomaston had not proved profitable, and he decided to leave it in the hands of his associates, Ballard Green in Thomaston and Peter Green, in Bath. He planned to lease the Stonehouse farm to Rufus Berry the next year, for $500 and half the taxes, and hoped it would be successful. He sold and rented some of his property in Bath for cash, and made provisions for his mill and establishment in Kingfield.

When King received official word of his four-year appointment, he wrote a letter dated May 27, 1821, to the committee members who had nominated him for governor, announcing his intention of withdrawing from office to become one of the commissioners for settling claims of American shipowners and merchants against Spain. He said he was not leaving for selfish reasons, he would decline the commission otherwise, "but unfortunate claimants in this part of the country ask me in the most feeling manner to accept. They fear if I decline another person may not be accepted from this State."[1]

On the 28th King formally resigned and William D. Williamson, the President of the Senate, took his place as governor. Six months later, Williamson was elected to Congress and Mr. Benjamin Ames, Speaker of the House, took his place until Albion Parris was elected to the office.

On the last day of May, William wrote to P. C. Brooks that he intended to come to Boston in a day or two, where he could board a packet for Washington. He wanted to consult Brooks on his method of evaluating vessels and also to see Henry Orne, who was to represent some of the claimants for damage under the treaty. This was to be a new experience for King.

It was with both pride and sadness that Ann helped William pack his bags and saw him off on the stage for Boston; proud that he had been accepted by the President to serve as a commissioner and sad, because it meant separation from his family for long periods of time. She in turn was left with the responsibility of their home and children, as well as keeping in touch with the business in Bath.

William was by nature fearless in pursuit of principles he considered right, therefore it was with confidence that he left Maine for the larger turmoil of Washington. He found that his fellow commissioners, Judge Hugh L. White from Kentucky and Littleton W. Tazewell of Virginia, were delegates with whom he could agree.

Judge Hugh L. White had been a justice of the Supreme Court of Tennessee from 1801 to 1807, and from 1809 to 1817. He had also served as U.S. District Attorney in 1808. Littleton W. Tazewell was a member of the Virginia House of Delegates from 1796 to 1800, and a congressman the following year. He had heartily supported the War of 1812, and had been appointed a commissioner to Spain in 1819 under the Treaty for the purchase of Florida. The three commissioners were to stay at Mrs. Peyton's place while working on the Commission. King's brother Rufus, pleased with William's appointment, sent him a long letter outlining the historical background of the Spanish Treaty, to enlarge his knowledge of the claims they were to judge, and William studied it carefully.

Engaged as he was in the problems of the Commission, William neglected to write to Ann. In a letter written the last of June, she told him of this fact. She informed him that his ship in Bath was almost loaded and the building was being completed. In regard to the coming election in Maine, she said that Mr. Sprague of Hallowell had visited her and told her that the upriver people were supporting General Chandler for governor, but the Bath people were for Wingate. She had heard from a friend that the Wingates were saying that King was working against them, and had noticed a decided coolness on meeting a number of ladies in town. On the surface, however, Colonel Wingate had been friendly. He had offered her a seat in Marsden's carriage with some other ladies, but, she wrote, "I've not decided. I'm too proud to depend on them for conveyance."[2] She was anxious for him to come home to discuss the situation with him.

King knew the Wingates were not the only ones who felt he had disappointed them both in Maine and in Washington. Nathan Ames had written him a long letter complaining of his "abuses" in not giving him a promised appointment.

Not long after receiving Ann's letter, William came home. He was in Bath when he received further knowledge that there was some truth in the rumors she had heard. Sam Cone sent him a copy of an anonymous letter sent to William's friend Albion Parris, candidate for governor of Maine, and asked King whether he thought it had come from the Wingates.

Bath, Jun. 29, 1821

To Judge Parris
Sir; Permit me (an old man) to give you a few seasonable hints — with regret I have noticed your name made mention of as candidate for governor and that too in opposition to the worthy and respectable Gen. Wingate — depend on it, you fail, if nominated. I know of only 3 persons *in this town* who will give you their suffrages, vis, Gov. King, and his *two* creatures, Col Robinson & Green, with the combined influence they may possibly obtain 7 *others*. The votes stand Wingate 450, Parris 10 — for your sake may God grant that the next Argus may announce that you are not a candidate.

signed (an old man)

At first King was not too concerned about these stories and the letter. He had personal business to attend to in Bath, Thomaston, and Kingfield. He was anxious, too, to gain support in Maine for William H. Crawford as the Democrat candidate for President. This gave his enemies a chance to get back at him. In August he received news from J. Seaver telling him that vicious stories were being circulated about him in the contest for the new governor. Wingate was implicated as saying King had money from the Spanish claims to pay his debts and had borrowed $27,000 and bartered away the vote of the state to Mr. Crawford.

These untrue stories and the letter did not help Wingate. Albion Parris won the election and became governor of Maine for the next five years. However, this was not to be the end of Wingate's feud with King.

Meanwhile William was back in Washington with a list of claims to help process. Concerning this interlude in King's life, a columnist on the *Bath Daily Times* who came across two papers among King's effects "that have been saved but have not seen the light of day for fifty years or more," copied them for the benefit of Bath readers in the Tuesday Evening Edition, April 4, 1906. The first one is a bill tendered in 1821 by Jesse Brown of the Indian Queen Hotel, Washington City. It can be seen that Governor King, who was in favor of Prohibition for the town of Bath, abided by his principles abroad as well as at home — also that he did not always stay at Mrs. Peyton's place.

Indian Queen Hotel
Washington City   Gov. King to Jesse Brown, Dr. 1821

June 7, to dinner, supper and lodging	$1.50
June 8, to postage	.54
June 9 to lemonade	.25
June 11 to lemonade	.25
June 12 to lemonade and cider	.62
June 13 to cider and lemonade	.62
June 14 to lemonade and punch,	.25
Board 7 days	10.50
Stage fare	4.00
	19.18

Received payment,
H. *Rumpff.*

The second paper consisted of an undated text in King's handwriting of a "proposed liquor traffic prohibitory law for the town of Bath":

> Whereas the expenses of the poor of this town have the last year increased to an alarming extent, so much so as to render this expense, with the other necessary expenses of the town, almost beyond the ability of the people to meet — and whereas the magistrates with many other citizens of the town, have made the increased expenses a subject of inquiry, the result of which having satisfied that the increased expense is to be attributed in a great measure to the too free use of ardent spirits, to remedy which evil, so injurious to the community and particularly to the deluded persons themselves, it is the duty of the town in its corporate capacity provided it is in its power to:

> Vote that it is considered particularly the duty of the selectmen to withhold their recommendations for license from all persons (retailers) who shall after this day sell to any person or inhabitant of this town liquors to be drank in their stores, or who shall sell in any quantity whatever spirits to such persons as the said selectmen or relatives of the persons may request them to decline selling to.

At this time, Ann, at home with the responsibility of the children and care of home affairs, was subject to more cool treatment. Stories on both sides made her uneasy and so disturbed her that she wrote to William in September and asked him what she should do. Others advised him of Ann's dilemma. King wrote to Ann to plan a party and invite the Wingates and others to it. Ann did as he suggested and wrote back:

> After I received your last letter, I felt priveleged to call on Mrs. Wingate (and) friends, and invite them to see me. I likewise invited many others, and made a plesant party. everything went on well — I understood that Conl Wingate would not attend owing to observation, made to him that he was trying to purchase your favour but I made it known to Mrs. W. that if he had any scruples I certainly should not return her visit therefore he came and the time passed pleasantly. I have received many delicate marks of attention from them for which they are entitled to my gratitude. . . .[4]

Ann had smoothed feelings somewhat, but King's troubles were not over, for there was still resentment over loss of appointments for which he was blamed.

While in Washington, he was much in the company of William Crawford, at that time secretary of the treasury. King agreed with him politically and felt that he would be a better President than John Quincy Adams, a Federalist. The *Eastern Argus* came out strongly for Crawford, too, arguing that he was a man of the people, whereas Adams was not. But most of the members of the Maine Legislature, although not openly endorsing Adams, favored him in spite of the efforts King made to persuade them to vote for Crawford.

King favored nominations of candidates by congressional caucus because Crawford had more supporters in Congress. In 1823, however, Crawford had a stroke and it was doubtful that he would be able to hold public office. The following February, when the last Republican caucus to meet was called to order, it was so unpopular that only 66 of the 216 Republicans in Congress attended. (The Republicans had dropped the prefix Democrat by this time.) Thereafter nominations were to be made by state legislatures.

Though unable to attend the meeting because of his paralysis, Crawford received all but four votes. Albert Gallatin received fifty-seven votes for Vice President and William King one.

According to Louis Hatch: "The caucus then issued an address to the people, which was drafted by John Holmes (of York) and revised by Martin Van Buren. It was very Republican in tone, and expressed a fear of 'the entire dismemberment of the party to which it is our pride to be attached.' "[5]

King was faced with an entirely new kind of politician. He was not happy with the address. He wrote his nephews in confidence that it was

> against the opinions and wishes of a great majority of Crawford's best friends and supporters in and out of the caucus, and misrepresented the sentiments of the man that it was put forth to serve; that it placed him (King) in a most unpleasant predicament at home. . . . where he had uniformly, and not without authority, asserted, that Mr. Crawford's course in conducting the affairs of the government would be tolerant of all sects and parties; that the principles contained in the address could be explained, it was true, but the necessity of resorting to this humiliating office might well have been spared, seeing that New York and Pennsylvania alone could respond to the doctrine of party contained in it.[6]

In the presidential election, John Quincy Adams won. He had pledged to appoint men without regard to party, and he kept his word. He treated men who had supported Crawford courteously and requested Crawford to stay in office as secretary of the treasury. He kept his word with members of the former Federalist Party, too, and appointed Rufus King minister to Great Britain in 1825. These offers smoothed ruffled feelings. Rufus, accompanied by his son, the newly appointed secretary of legation, went to England, but due to illness stayed only a year before he had to come home. He died in

1827, a great loss to his family and the nation. Rufus's son James wrote to his Uncle William telling of his father's death, saying that all but Edward, who was in Ohio, were with him at home.

During the presidential campaign of 1824 the old (Democrat) Republican Party that King had hoped would create good feelings and sponsor economic measures for better business conditions, broke up. At this time King's duties on the Spanish Claims Commission were over, and he left Washington to return to Bath, his home, and business. He found himself in a bitter controversy with Nathan Ames and Joseph F. Wingate.

Ames, candidate for renomination for government office, and Wingate, candidate for renomination for collector of the port of Bath, had been nominated by President Monroe in 1823. They expected the aid of King to secure renomination but failed to obtain his influence. "The rejection of Ames by the Senate was unanimous. Wingate received only one vote. It was said by General King that their defeat was occasioned 'for their having been engaged in trade with the enemy during the war, as well as for other reasons.' "[7] The other reasons might have been the lies and vicious stories told about King and his friends during the state elections.

Wingate and Ames did not feel any better toward King when his friend Mark L. Hill was given the post of collector of the port of Bath. In 1824, soon after King returned to Bath, an anonymous pamphlet was printed, charging him with illicit trading during the Embargo and War of 1812. It contained affidavits and copies of letters, from captains who had sailed on King's vessels, to prove he was engaged in illicit trade.

King, supported by Mark L. Hill, replied with a pamphlet denying the statements and showing the unreliability of some of the shipmasters who had been in his employ; two of whom he stated had stolen both vessel and cargo and having sold them kept the proceeds. He made a point of the fact that the captains of the vessels who took the oath at the Customs House on arrival home that their vessels had been to neutral ports, and in their affidavits in Ames's pamphlet testified that their voyages had been to prohibited ports, were as guilty as they said King was for taking false oaths. A number of captains whose afidavits accused King of illicit trading took back their previous statements. King accused Ames and some of his friends of illicit trading in return and listed his own vessels tied up during this time and the losses he suffered because of it.

His general defense of his trading (confirmed by a study of his letters), was:

> In conducting my merchantile business I was influenced, by the advice of the best informed political men, that, as soon as Congress assembled, the non-intercourse system would be abandoned by a declaration of war against France or England, or by adopting some other measure. Availing myself of this information, I gave my vessels a direction accordingly. The information in regard to a declaration of war proved correct, with the exception of its not having been declared as soon as was contemplated. The Reunion, which returned before the war, was seized and condemned for having been to a prohibited port; no claim was made on my part; the vessel was sold and I was the purchaser.[8]

All this controversy only hurt the reputations of both parties and did nothing to help anyone. The Ames controversy caused Mark L. Hill to lose his position as collector of customs in Bath and the appointment of John B. Swanton in his place. That King was not injured by these assaults on his trading career is shown by his appointment as customs collector in Bath four years later in 1829.

XII

KING turned his attention to town, state, and family affairs after his return from Washington. The political controversy quieted down and Bath people who had sympathized with those who had defied the law during the war that restricted their trade did not severely criticize King. The town was growing and new businesses competed with his. Actually at that time, according to Henry Owen:

> ... Commerce was of greater importance than shipbuilding. The increasing, locally owned fleet was engaged in both domestic and foreign carrying to the enrichment not only of the owners, but of the whole town. Bath itself was a busy port, with arrivals averaging in 1824 about 70 per month, ten per cent of them from foreign ports, chiefly the West Indies. These brought the goods for an extensive wholesale and retail trade conducted by the Bath merchants. The loading and unloading of these craft, and their provisioning, outfitting and repair, and the wages of their crews contributed largely to local profit.
> It was at this period that several of the greatest Bath shipping houses, whose reputation was to become international, were founded. Levi Houghton had launched his first brig, the Bolton, as lately as 1819 in the former Davis shipyard. George F. and John Patten, who began their career as shipbuilders and shipowners in

Topsham, launched their first vessel in Bath in 1821. William D. Sewall, when he launched his brig Diana in 1823, had laid the corner stone of the great shipbuilding and ship operating career of his family. Johnson Rideout and Johnson Williams both began building in 1825. Oliver and William V. Moses came to town respectively in 1825 and 1826. . . .[1]

King was intensely interested in the welfare of his chosen city. A notice in the paper in 1825 shows his interest in fire protection:

> Joseph Sewall, secretary, gives notice of a meeting of the firewards Apr. 11 at the house of William King at which the duties were apportioned as follows:
> William King, Samuel Davis and Jonathan Hyde to have general superintendence and direction at fires, to examine the buildings on fire and those in the vicinity, and with the assent of the firewards present to give such orders and directions as the exigencies of the case may require.
> John Richardson, Luke Lambard and Zabdiel Hyde to be attached to and have the care of Engine No. 1.
> David Stinson, James McLellan and Samuel Winter, same with respect to No. 2.
> Charles Crawford to manage fire hook No. 1.
> Nathaniel Weld, fire hook No. 2.
> Charles Clapp, Ebenezer Clapp, William Richardson, Daniel Marston and Joseph Sewall to take charge of property, buildings and furniture exposed at fires and secure the same.[2]

This attempt at fire protection no doubt helped to prevent fires that happened later from spreading beyond their immediate areas.

King was interested in better streets and transportation for the Point. He made plans for a bridge at the foot of Center Street and another along his dock at the foot of Elm Street, which he finished in 1829, uniting the Point with other parts of town to improve business on Front Street.

Ann and the children were happy to have William at home. He brought life to the house with visitors and parties for the children and grownups. One of the children's playmates recalled many years later a party she attended at the King mansion. Mrs. A. S. Swasey wrote:

I remember so well the old Governor, his courtly presence, his heavy brow, and overhanging eye-brows, and searching eyes, his firm mouth which so readily softened into a smile, as he took the hand of a little child. And beside him, the slight but stately figure of his wife, whose soft voice and kindly care in entertaining us did so much to make our visit pleasant. The old mansion was a perfect treasure house of enjoyment. . . .

The long dining room was at the end of the hall. Whether it was really *very* large, I have no idea. I only know its proportions seem vast to me, as I look back upon a table in the center, around which gathered half-a-dozen happy children, and from which it seemed a long journey to the high bookcases at the upper end, crowded with substantially bound volumes.

The windows of the dining-room opened to the floor on to a veranda leading to the garden, where grew plum, cherry, apple and pear trees.

In one corner of the garden, almost hidden by its vines — woodbine and grapevine — stood a summer house, somewhat out of repair, and sadly needing a coat of paint, as my maturer judgment tells me. But then it was a bower of beauty to us, and held within it many a merry group; and to this day it stands to me as the embodiment of its kind. For, whenever I read a story in which a summer house is described, the picture which always arises before me is just like this, as it looked in Gov. King's garden on those happy summer afternoons.

But the greatest attraction of all was an old disused coach, standing in the stable, which, after the delights of exploration within doors were exhausted, was a never failing source of enjoyment. Whether the family ever had used it, or whether it had descended from some more remote time of majesty, I know not. It was old, and faded, and worn. I imagine the springs had lost all their elasticity years before, and the gaily painted outside had parted with its pristine glory. But no matter! With unbounded delight we climbed the rickety steps, and seated ourselves upon the leathern cushions, and gave reins to the steeds of our imaginations.

Not alone to children were the hospitalities of the King mansion enjoyable; for we often lingered around the breakfast tables of our homes to listen to the stories told by our fathers and mothers, of the sociable tea-drinking, or the brilliant party of the evening before, given by the Governor and his wife, entertainments which were always pronounced to be the most complete in all the graces of cultured festivity that society in Bath afforded in those days.[3]

In the summer there were delightful rides for Ann and the children, when William took them to Kingfield. A picnic lunch was packed for the family, and frequent stops were made along the way to visit and rest. When they arrived they were welcomed by the caretakers of the new house King had had built in 1821, and cousins they had not seen since the year before. Ann and Mary Elizabeth stayed at the house, but Cyrus William, too active to rest, went with his father and played with the boys in the fields, while his father inspected his farm and mills. Before leaving, there was always a feast from the products of the farm, which William especially enjoyed. Another picnic lunch was prepared for their return home, and more stops were made along the way until they arrived in Bath, tired and happy.

However, a depression was building up at this time. Owen states:

> Beginning in 1827, according to Lemont, 'no vessels were built in Bath for some time.' That is not quite borne out by the Custom House records, but building slackened considerably. Lemont states that carpenters were obliged to seek work in St. John, N.B., but finding little to do there, came back and worked for 50 to 75 cents a day, taking store pay, working from daylight to dark, and employed only occasionally at that. . . .[4]

Ann and William had had some happy times with their children, but in 1828 King had to come to a decision about his son, Cyrus William. Ann was becoming increasingly tired with the care of Mary Elizabeth, whose frequent and continued convulsions were a constant worry. Cyrus, active and headstrong, had become hard to manage. Bath port, though not as busy as it had been in 1824, was still a dangerous place for a little boy, even in this period of depression. No amount of scolding or warning seemed to keep him off the wharf and river front. He would not obey his mother and had all sorts of excuses to explain his absences.

King had been appointed commissioner of public building in Maine in 1827 and was expecting to be away from home while he was superintending the building of the State House in Augusta, either there, or consulting the architect Charles Bulfinch in Boston. It was going to be a big job, for the building was to follow a reduced plan of St. Peter's Church in Rome. It was King's responsibility to furnish the building as well.* This was something he felt he could do; but coping with a small boy was beyond him. He was becoming more irritated with the child every day, for his lack of good behavior and obedience, which was adding another burden to Ann. Finally he talked with Cyrus William and persuaded him to go to Mr. Wells's School for Moral Discipline in South Boston for a year.

It saddened Ann to see her beloved son go away to school, but knowing how he exasperated his father and feeling he would be safer where he would have good training and the supervision that she could not give him, she consented to let him go. The children she had looked forward to for so long had become a burden and worry to their father. Cyrus would be better off in Boston.

Cyrus, unused to strict discipline, was not happy there. After some two years he wrote a pleading letter to his father:

South Boston, Sept. 4 (1830)

My dear Father,

I suppose you know that for some time past, I have been rather discontented with this school. And I tell you frankly that I am very much so. I do not learn so fast as I wish to. I do not have half the attention that I wish to have paid to me and I do think that while I remain here it is lost time, for I only study those lessons that I am obliged to get. I do not go out doors to play but only to exercise. I do not associate more than I can help with the boys for I am the oldest in the school and am not fond of associating with so small boys. I do not like to have boys younger than myself tell me to do so and so, order me about; stop my talking, stand me out from exercise and therefore loose my dinner. I have been here now nearly two years and when I first came here you only wished me to remain here one year which I very willingly did. Since that I have told you that I wished to leave the school for several reasons.

---

*The building and its furnishings cost the state $125,000, a sum considered extravagant by King's critics.

I do think I am too large and old to be governed by boys younger than myself. I have had it so long and now can have it no longer. The rules of the school command the boys to obey the monitors. But, from the time I receive an answer to this letter I will not be ordered about by the monitors. I will be expelled first for I cannot be treated so. I have told you in some of my other letters how that Mr. Wells had degraded me to the 2nd grade where I have to hold up my hand when I wish to speak in school time. I have but 10¢ a week and I do not think that I ought to have been degraded. Mr. Wells has said that I must not go to the city. I cannot even pass from the shore or bathing house without I am with some monitor or by Mr. Wells particular permission.

I will not trouble you with any more of my troubles except to ask you as a father to remove me from the school for I am sure it will prevent further trouble and Mr. Wells expects to visit England this Fall therefore I shall return then and what is a month here. It is nothing but vexation to me. I love Mr. Wells and respect the family but do not like to be governed by some of his rules. He says himself that in some respects his school is much stricter than West Point School therefore you can judge a little of the treatment I receive and a good deal from boys younger than myself. I ask you as a boy in distress. Will you give me something to quench my parching thirst? *Will you* grant me one request *which is to remove me from the school?* I do not wish to remain in Bath. Place me anywhere you please and I will be contented. Answer me by return mail in boat as I wish to hear as soon as possible and I pray that you will grant me the only request which I have here asked you to. WILL YOU REMOVE ME FROM THIS SCHOOL? I pray you do.

From your son
C. W. King[5]

King evidently did not think he should send Cyrus to another school. Though Cyrus may have come home on some vacations, he continued on at the Boston school, but with fewer complaints, probably because Mr. Wells must have given him a monitoring job. Later he took Cyrus on as an assistant.

Meanwhile Washington politics continued at its own pace.

Political maneuvering on the part of Jackson's southern

supporters gave him the presidency, through what became known as the "tariff of abominations," which backfired throughout the nation.

> The Southerners were not strong enough to keep a new high tariff bill out of Congress in 1828, but they resorted to a shrewd trick to defeat it. Instead of seeking to lower the tariff rates proposed, they joined with the Western farmers in greatly increasing them. A presidential election was approaching, and the South appealed to a large anti-Adams sentiment to frame a tariff bill so preposterous that New England would reject it, and so bring dishonor and defeat upon Adams's cause. For example, New England wanted a high duty on manufactured woolens to exclude English goods, but at the same time it wanted cheap raw wool for its factories. It wanted a high duty on cordage to protect its shipbuilding industries, but it wanted cheap raw hemp for its ropewalks. It wanted a high duty on iron manufactures, but cheap pig iron for its forges. All New England's demands for protection to manufactures were granted in their bill, but their benefits were largely neutralized by the addition of high duties on raw wool to please the sheep raisers of Ohio, on hemp to satisfy the farmers of Kentucky, and on pig iron to conciliate the miners of Pennsylvania. In spite of this shrewd plan of the South to match the West against New England, and thus please nobody by pleasing everybody, the fantastic bill passed the House by a vote of 105 to 94, the Senate by a vote of 26 to 21, and became a law by President Adams's signature (May 19, 1828). It was a low political job, which, as Randolph said, "had to do with no manufactures except the manufacture of a president."

Maine suffered particularly from the new tariff. "Among the 'abominations' was one doubling the duty on molasses, and thus striking a heavy blow at the West India trade. Maine lumber, Maine ships, and all the industries dependent on them, were seriously affected. When the news that the bill had passed reached Portland, the town went into mourning. Stores were hung with crepe, bells were tolled, and the vessels in the harbor half-masted their flags."[7]

In 1829 King was appointed collector of customs for the port of Bath, and began his duties on the second floor of the Bath Bank. He was located across the street from his home, store, and wharf. While he was in Washington, his associates Peter H. Green and Judge

Porter had looked after his interests in the bank and store, with occasional visits from him, and would continue to do so under his supervision while he was busy in the customs office.

John Bosworth had taken over the shipyard. According to an item in the *Maine Gazette* March 29, 1824, he "threatens with 'Linche's Law' persons coming to his shipyard to take chips or other articles." King had given up the thought of building another vessel since they had built the *Ann* in 1810 and his ship the *Visitor* in 1815; instead, he had acquired the *Asia* and *Ganges* from the Marine Insurance Company in Wiscasset in 1818, and was not planning then to invest any more money in ships. His vessels were getting old and often in need of repairs, but were still carrying lumber and farm products, to which he had added Kennebec ice, to the southern states and the West Indies. He was finding it difficult to get paying cargoes for the return voyages.

By 1830 the new young and energetic group of men who had entered shipping were building larger, swifter sailing vessels and founding businesses in Bath that would end in making their houses internationally known long after King's business was forgotten. During the first three years of this third decade of the century, 63 vessels of increasing size were built, and the *New England*, 549 tons, built in 1833, held the local record for size up to that time. With his already dwindling fortune, King could not expect to compete with them. He felt he should stay close to his business in Bath and be near Ann when she needed him.

In 1830 Mrs. Elizabeth Fields, a widow of Robert Fields, an English lawyer who resided in Boston, came to visit the Kings. To entertain her they took her on a ride to Topsham, and as they passed the Doctor Porter house, King pointed it out as his sister Betsy's home, now his, the Porters having moved to Camden in 1829, when his business association with his brother-in-law ended. The house, however, because of its size and cost was likely to remain empty, he thought.

Mrs. Fields fell in love with the house and suggested to King that she would like to take possession of it for a boarding school for young ladies. King was enthusiastic about the idea and after making the necessary arrangements with him, Mrs. Fields opened her school in 1831 with twelve boarding scholars and as many day scholars. King was delighted to send Mary Elizabeth there and used his influence to have his friends in Augusta and elsewhere send their daughters, too. The school was very successful and when Mrs. Fields gave it up in 1844, Miss Hester Hinckley continued it.

Mary Elizabeth was not able to go to the school for very long, however, according to a letter written by Ann Frazier Bridge to her sister, Mary Caroline, after Mary Elizabeth visited her for a fortnight in the spring of 1832:

> She has had convulsion fits since she had the scarlet fever last spring. . . . She is not allowed to study, reads a little for amusement, rides, plays chess, backgammon, cards, plays on the piano, & draws some, cuts paper for candle ornaments very beautifully, she looks most of the time in good health — her spirits are generally good, is a good deal with her young companions particularly Harriet Richardson. This winter her fits have been more frequent — about once a fortnight, but not so violent as some she has had. — Her friends fear very much it may injure her intellect, but from her age, and strict diet, Physicians think she may recover. She does not sew any. It is a great affliction to Uncle & Aunt . . . Aunt has lost a great deal of flesh & her countenance is changed, Uncle Will'm has been in town considerable.[8]

Ann Bridge and her sister visited the Kings as often as they could and sometimes took Mary Elizabeth to visit with them to give her mother some rest.

With the disappointment of not being able to send Mary Elizabeth to school and loss of hope that her health would ever improve, Ann and William's hope for her future ended. It was a heavy burden they would carry until she died.

XIII

THE decline of King's power in business and politics began in the 1830s. The failure of President Adams to establish good trade with the British West Indies had reduced the profit from southern trade. The Tariff of Abominations had cut still further into the possibility of profit from shipping. King felt there was little hope for better business under President Jackson's administration.

In 1832 his business suffered another loss. His Bath Bank's charter expired and was not renewed. Jackson had vetoed the bill for renewing the charters of the banks of the United States, because he believed they catered to businessmen and that the officers in the banks opposed him in politics.

King, as director of the Maine Bank of the United States in Bath, as well as owner of the Bath Bank, sensed a widespread panic with the destruction of the nation's banks. The generous amount of money Secretary Crawford had deposited in his bank was ordered withdrawn, and since there was not enough cash available to pay the whole amount at once, King and the directors had to draw on their own savings to pay the difference.

King was not reappointed to the office of collector of customs in 1834, for Jackson believed a friend and supporter should be appointed instead. That same year, the bank being closed, the United States acquired King's bank building, which was sold to the Sagadahoc Bank in 1859.

Disgusted with Jackson's policies, King joined the National Republicans, who were called Whigs. They had an excellent organization and asked King to preside over their convention. They nominated Peleg Sprague for governor of Maine, but he did not win the election. A strong anti-Masonic feeling existed throughout Maine at this time. Many thought that Masons belonged to the educated, wealthier class of people who would take over the government and run it for themselves, but though some may have been influenced by this, it was not made an issue in this election.*

There was some criticism of the Democrats on their use of the English language by Senator John Holmes, who had also joined the Whigs. The *Eastern Argus*, backing the Democrats, came back at the Whigs by bringing up King's poor spelling on papers of instruction in the War of 1812. Fearing big business and the power of the banks, however, the people elected Democrat Robert P. Dunlap, a prominent Mason, for governor.

In 1835 the Whigs made another attempt to gain control of the state government. This time they adopted the policy of promoting internal improvements, and according to Hatch:

> The Maine Whigs now declared that the State should adopt the policy, and nominated ex-Governor King, who they hoped might win some Democrat votes (from his former Republican friends). The Democrats renominated Governor Dunlap and met their opponents firmly but not without some apprehension and a slight tendency to "hedge." The *Argus* said that the *Advertiser* (the Whig paper) urged King's election mainly on the ground that he favored internal improvements, and would if chosen be a De Witt Clinton — but that "we never heard before of General King's enthusiasm for internal improvement."[1]

This was a slur on King's superintending the construction of the State House in Augusta and its cost.

The *Argus* went on to say that the Federalists, as it called the Whigs, "meant to put their principles out of sight and endeavor to float their candidate into office upon the temporary tide of internal

---

* It is interesting to note that after many years of slander and abuse, starting as early as 1829, by 1849 there were 994 Masons in Maine.

improvements. Perhaps it would be a more just figure to say the Federalists contemplated running General King into the chair of state upon a railroad."[2] In spite of their sarcasm, King himself had already done much to improve transportation with roads and bridges in his own area and was still interested in improving conditions throughout the state.

The Democrats in Maine agreed with President Jackson in his determination to do away with the United States banks. Maine voters showed by their vote this time that they feared debt for internal improvements and also corporations with money and power. The vote for Dunlap was 45,608 and for King 18,680, with a scattering vote of 90.

King had learned that he no longer could swing political weight to improve the business situation. The next year he refused to be a candidate. He was through with politics and never would run for office again. By now he had serious personal business difficulties to contend with.

Even in Bath where he had been called the "Sultan," King found people, especially the younger generation, resentful of his dominance of many years in town affairs. A story from Reed's *History of Bath* illustrates this:

> . . . A club of young men, the Zetetic Club, was formed in contradistinction to a lyceum of older and more conservative men, and the members, after a long discussion of the education question, prepared to act in concert at an annual town meeting on a measure to be offered to improve the schools. It was arranged to proceed in this wise: An order, prefaced by suitable remarks, was to be offered by a member designated, to raise for schools an additional sum of $3000 more than was required by law to do, and consequently would provoke strong opposition from large tax payers. It was arranged that a dozen or so should be ready to reply in turn to the opposition, and that they should be well distributed in the house so as not to appear to act in concert. Town meeting was held and the "order" offered, and immediately assailed by General King, who did not make any lengthy remarks, seeming to be confident, as he had always before "carried the town," that it was only necessary to make known his wishes to have them fully

carried out. To his manifest surprise, however, no sooner had he taken his seat than a vigorous reply was made to his remarks by the man who had offered the order and between whom and King there had been some previous sparring on some other question. To effectually silence him, King arose, looking straight at his opponent, with the remark that he "would willingly favor the appropriating more money for the support of schools if it would result in preventing children of some men from being as ignorant as their fathers have shown themselves here today." No sooner was the general seated when another advocate of the measure was on his feet in a distant part of the room, presuming to antagonize the long-time dictator. Amazed at this audacity, General King rose again and with more extended remarks apparently thought he had silenced the reformers. Then a voice from a far corner of the house is heard, dashing aside his arguments with audacity. Again General King takes the floor, and no sooner is he seated than Robert Babb assails him and evidently pitches into his feelings to some purpose. King inquires of those around him, "who is he?" and arising with glaring eyes looking around the room, says he: "Mr. Moderator, I should like to know what we are coming to! Who is this Mr. Roberty, Bobberty Babb, and the rest of them, are they going to rule the town?" The other members continuing to reply and assail him, General King, thoroughly amazed at this audacity, inquired of a neighbor what it all meant, "this happening in such a manner," and he arose in his mighty indignation to say: "Ah, Mr. Moderator, I have just learned where all this mischief comes from; it is the Zetetic Club; and what do we see?" pointing with his finger, "Why its a cockadodle here, and its a cockadodle there, and its a cockadodle everywhere; and what does it all mean?"[3]

The "Cockadodles," unsympathetic with the financial and business worries of King, however, carried their point with the complete overthrow of his rule.

Beginning in the 1790s, King's real estate deals had been numerous. He had land in Scarborough, farms in Topsham, Bowdoinham and Litchfield. Outside of his property on the Point, he had bought land along the waterfront, and land, farms, and buildings in North Bath, West Bath, Line's Island, Arrowsic, Georgetown, Phippsburg, and Thomaston, as well as in some other parts of the District. The details of most of his transactions are to be found today in the Lincoln County Courthouse in Wiscasset, then Bath's county seat.

Because of his financial dificulties, King had to sell most of his properties, but he had faith in and held on to the one that contributed most to his ruin, and that was his "Million Acre Farm," in Kingsfield.

For a number of years King had been building up a little community in his holdings. He was so pleased with the good farming land there that he sent his nephew, Rufus Porter, son of Betsy and Dr. Benjamin Jones Porter, to Kingfield to help manage his affairs and to pick out a good farm for himself. Nathaniel Dudley, King's agent there, tutored Rufus in the business and helped him get established to work with him. In the meantime, Rufus acquired a farm. He met, fell in love with, and married Ruth Knapp, whose father gave him title to his farm in Kingfield.

Neither Dudley nor Rufus Porter could make the venture pay for King. Many who came there to take up farms were without money and unused to farming in the wilderness, they soon gave up their holdings. Some proved dishonest and greedy and infringed upon the rights of others. Death and hard luck plagued some, and they could not pay their debts. The agents were having a hard time to keep law and order and they lost control of some unruly settlers. Hard times that followed the loss of his bank made it impossible for King to go to Kingfield or to pay his taxes. In July of 1842 he received a letter from N. D. Richardson on his farm saying: "Albee Parsons, Collector of taxes for 1841 cald here today and said that he must have the tax that is due in town from you which he says is something like 70 or 80 Dollars which he must have 35 Dollars in one week from next Wednesday or he will take the stock on the farm and sell it at Auction. He will advertise in one week from Thursday next if you are not coming up by that time send 35 Dollars and he will wait for a remainder untill you come. . . ."[4]

Whether king was able to send the money or not is not revealed in his files. Deane Dudley, who continued his interest in King, wrote:

> I fear his hopes in regard to the increase of his estates there (in Kingfield) were never fully realized. The tide of emigration

began to set strongly toward the west. Mount Abraham lost many of its attractions for seekers of new lands. Nevertheless, for many years subsequent to the first above mentioned date (1842) Gov. King took hearty pleasure in his own Kingfield. There was one thing that seems strange in so great a man (may the readers pardon me for mentioning it), he never dispensed any gratuities among us boys. I think it probable he was an economical gentleman. In further proof of this I am able to state that I used to see him, and even later, hasten down to his wharf in Bath, as soon as our little steamer, *Minerva* would arrive, to collect his own wharfage. His house was in full view of the wharf. But this labor may have been performed for exercise.

The last time I ever saw the gallant and distinguished old governor was when he had become an octogenarian. I passed his residence one fine day as he was watering his garden. He never knew me, or at least, noticed me, as I remember, in his life, yet it was not that he would have deemed me unworthy, perhaps, to write this sketch, but such was his dignified, somber mood, and way of life.[5]

In 1842 King's vessels were no longer sailing and bringing in profit. High tariffs and a business depression had reduced his capital, and the loss of his bank and his government office had left him financially unable to conduct business outside his wharf and store. It seems that J. F. Anderson was half right about his hastening to the wharf, for King was anxious to collect all that was due him, and was probably not collecting his own wharfage for the exercise. Anderson's observation that King was economical seems to have been accurate.

King wanted to get the most out of a transaction that he could without spending too much money on it. He never wanted anything extra paid out on his vessels, other than what was necessary to keep them sailing. He had not wanted to pay extra money on board and traveling for Ann to come to Boston, preferring to stay at a cheaper boarding place than she would have liked; yet he loved his wife and came home as often as his business allowed.

He invested in farms, lands and lots, with the thought of making a bargain or some money on them and at times tied up his extra cash in his deals. He often was slow in paying his bills, but when his associates reminded him of this, he seemed to find the money and have some left for further deals.

King had spent some of his own money in the War of 1812, but he was fighting to protect his District then with the hope that he and his fellow businessmen might sail again, free to trade without interference. He was not above using the enemies' resources to accomplish his aims and keep his vessels sailing for trade. He spent time and money traveling with the purpose in mind of freeing his District from Massachusetts and sponsoring his political party to create better business for all. Naturally commanding and forceful, he often rode rough-shod over his opponents. He was above cheating anyone and had no sympathy for those who did. His friends respected his original and sometimes profound thinking. Some who knew both William and his brother Rufus considered William the intellectual superior.

In 1843 King's income was so low that he asked William Richardson, his niece Harriet's husband, to take a mortgage on his home and land on the Point.

The previous November, Cyrus W. had written his father for permission to remain at Mr. Wells's School for Moral Discipline. He apparently did not even know that King was in such severe financial difficulty. The last letter we have from Cyrus reads:

S.M.D. Boston, Nov 11, 1842

My dear Father
    Last evening Mr. Wells informed me that if I liked he should like to have me remain and I have concluded to stop with him this winter. He furnishes my cloaths; board and washings and $1 a week.

    As mother said she should like to have me here I think I had better remain. I want to have you look out for me a situation in the spring if you can.

    Mr. Wells seems to like me and I think I can render him a good deal of assistance. Please remember me to all inquiring friends and if you can I wish you would send me 5 or 6 dollars.

I remain as ever yours
Cyrus Wm. King.

In 1847 Mary Elizabeth died. Shortly after this, King seemed to lose interest in things. He became forgetful and confused in his mind. When it seemed his mind was failing, William's affairs were put into the hands of Asa Redington, LLD. Ann, learning that her husband could not give Bowdoin College the $6,000 he had pledged for the new chapel, asked to have his named removed from it, but because King had done so much for Bowdoin, the name was retained.

Ann must have asked Cyrus William to come home before his father's affairs were taken over by Redington. He had been home and was attending Bowdoin Medical School by 1850. It seems sad that Cyrus William was not able to come to his father's assistance at this time, but William had had no patience with the boy and had not kept him close to him so that he could bring him up in the business. He might have been of real help to his father, had he been given the opportunity. Ann, who adored her sensitive and artistic son, had not felt her husband would accept any help from him, and now it was too late for anyone to restore the business.

The Million-Acre Farm was sold at auction on November 5, 1851, at Hapgood and Brown's Tavern in North Anson. Thirty thousand acres were sold in the towns of Kingfield, Lexington, and Concord. Thomas D. Robinson, King's Bath Bank treasurer, aided in the sale to salvage what he could for Ann and Cyrus William. Kingfield farm went to Mr. James Dolbier, whose wife Mary Ann Porter was Betsy and Dr. Benjamin Porter's granddaughter, thus in a way keeping it in the family.

On February 17, 1852, William Richardson having died, John D. and other heirs, on consideration of $11,000 paid by the United States Government, conveyed the premises "now occupied by General William King" to the government. This transaction took place five months before the death of General King, the residence, however, being reserved by the grantors.

XIV

WE learn of the final illness of William King from a letter written by Ann F. K. Bridge to her sister Hannah on June 9, 1852. She had come to see her Aunt Ann and while she was there, her aunt had had an ill turn so she stayed on to take care of her. Then her "Uncle King" was attacked with influenza. When he attempted to go to bed, he found that he had lost the use of his limbs. No one was aware that he had been exposed to influenza.

King remained in a lethargic state through the night. In the morning, Ann wrote:

> He was nearly as well as usual and remain'd so until a week since, excepting increased sleepiness and some coughing. Last Wednesday P.M. noticing he was quite feverish, I call'd in the attending physician. That night Miss Webber watch'd with him — his fever was higher next Day and that night Miss Covel and myself watch'd with him. (Miss Covel an excellent nurse). Since — his coughing has been constant night and day — but not rapid, which has of course weaken'd him very much — the last four or five days has refus'd all nourishment but liquids — can only set up to have his bed made as quick as possible — today he can't spit and we have to wipe the plegm out of his mouth — he is easily control'ed but not rational. — No continued sleep but a half an

hour or two between 4 and 10 A.M. An experienced man takes care of him nights. He once nursed Mr. John Richardson (who)... procur'd him for us... Within a week dear Mr. Fiske has been in and pray'd.

I'm now with dear Uncle. Miss Webber has gone down to attend to dinner. He does not appear to suffer except from weariness and coughing and oppression...

Dear Aunt is wonderfully better, continues gaining strength though anxious about Uncle — walks about the chambers, reads some, sews some, is often in Uncle's chamber — She has not even yet much appetite. Her only bodily troubles the last few days are palpitation along her left side, and for an hour (or) two is in the morning short of breath. She too was taken with the influenza, just after Uncle — but has entirely recovered....[1]

William King died at his home in Bath, June 17, 1852.

Some time later, Ann, knowing her sister Mary Caroline's deep religious convictions, wrote to her hoping to ease her feelings concerning their uncle's salvation.

Madison Aug 20, '52

Dear Sister

I feel rather tired writing but I've long wish'd to describe to you dear Uncle W. King's appearance the day before his decease; I promis'd it too when Olive was writing you from Saco — I thought her description very just for one who was not an eye witness — but mine ought to be — and perhaps may be more accurate. Mrs. Lombard once dear Aunt King's neighbour, and who has been in the habit of being much with her for years in her troubles, and myself, as Wednesday June 16th we were going up to dear Uncle's room from tea — concluded Aunt ought not again that night to go in there — it agitated her so much. Just after, we were alone with Uncle, when he who through the day had only discover'd short intervals of consciousness, turn'd his head and look'd most affectionately at Mrs. L. and took her hand — we had noticed his sight was growing dim and I told her he mistook her for Aunt, and I would go and bring Aunt in. When he had Aunt's hand, he appear'd still more pleased. We were all weeping for joy as an assistant came up, and said the Rev Mr Fiske was down stairs. Aunt said shall we ask him up. I told her by all means — and ran down and told him the scene we were just passing through. He said perhaps he better not go up — I said I came to carry him. When he first enter'd the room, he mentioned the afternoon of the day before, he could not help feeling some encouragement, for when he ask'd Uncle if he should pray with him — he answered he should have been very glad to have had him had he felt able and that when he went out, Uncle said "God bless you." Then he ask'd Uncle if he should pray with him — Uncle very earnestly but indistinctly said "yes"; while in his prayer he was speaking of the goodness of God — Uncle caught his hand from Aunt's, threw both arms in the air, and with a rapturous look upward, clapped them — and with a number of loud clappings — shouted like one experiencing a great and unexpected joy. We all exclaim'd with astonishment, joy and awe, for we all felt that God was indeed present in His power and grace. A few minutes after I ask'd Mr Fiske to speak to him of the joys of heaven — when there were the same gestures and expression of contenance, and joy — with less strength. I told Mr Fiske I had heard of such scenes, but had never expected to witness one — that I thought I had some faith in regard to Uncle — but the reality far surpass'd it. Dear Uncle had never appear'd so before, and after a restless night became insensible at four o'clock AM and continued so until a little after four o'clock P.M. when at his last breath I took my hand off his forehead. Uncle Redington arriv'd an hour before this — when he saw Uncle his face became very pale and solemn — and he slowly repeated "has it come to this" — Rev Mr Fiske had previously pray'd specially for Uncle King a number of times in Aunt's room — One afternoon I told Mr Fiske I wish'd his prayers to be made in his room — he went in and Miss Webber had the audacity to tell him she w'd not consent. Mr Fiske came and told me, in his wandering state of mind he did not know as it was essential — I remonstrated with Miss W and told her all things were possible with God and one word might sink deep in his mind; at any rate, that she was not his wife nor mistress of the family, and Aunt must decide. I ask'd Aunt, and she said perhaps it was as well to have the prayer in her room. I went out soon after and found the door of Uncle's room directly leading to Aunt's room fasten'd, I went round the other way, and told Miss W firmly, but gently and calmly to unfasten it — and she did. Indeed dear Sister I am thankful my heavenly Father open'd the way for me to be there nearly eleven weeks, for I really think I was needed. I went there with the determination to do everything for their welfare to the utmost strength of my body mind and heart — Then I could have no painful after reflections and truly I can say, I've nothing to reproach myself for. It is the greatest of comforts to think of dear Uncle as in heaven. I know not who could have witness'd the scene Wednesday P.M. and not believe he's there.

Just returned from a ride of six miles with Octavia — roads excellent, and through pleasant views. Mr Bridge told me Saturday his copies of Uncle King's funeral sermon had come, I told him to enclose one to you and Sister Haywood if he has not, I will when I return home — Am glad Sister Haywood has been gaventing around so much this season — think its time Sister Hale to begin — and please to do so by coming to our house soon — I shall expect you — you must be tired of Annie, hope she's on the point of starting off for Buffalo. Remember us to your good husband and children and write soon. Yes as ever

A. F. K. Bridge

P.S.
I think Uncle's friends individually may consider his salvation an answer to their prayers.[2]

The *Northern Tribune* a weekly paper published in Bath, on June 25, 1852, carried a page one obituary of Governor King:

A Great Man Has Fallen

Died at his residence in this city on Thursday, the 17th inst., Hon. William King, aged 84 years.

Notwithstanding a severe and protracted illness, has for several years past kept the deceased, in a great measure, secluded from the world, yet all recognize the fact that a great man has fallen.

The father, of the deceased, Richard King, Esq. was a merchant of note and respectability in the town of Scarboro in this State, which was also the native town of the illustrious individual whose decease it is now our painful duty to record.

William King was bereft of his father in early life. In common with many others of that time, he experienced the privations consequent upon the revolution.

His early education was comparatively neglected, and his

GENERAL WILLIAM KING 139

physical powers called into constant and vigorous exercise. About the year 1794 he removed to the town of Topsham, where he engaged in navigation and the manufacturing of lumber.

From Topsham he removed to this city about the year 1800. From that time until this he has been a resident of Bath.

In view of the active and important service rendered by the deceased to his fellow citizens and the country during his life, we presume all will concur in the opinion that he is the most distinguished man which Maine has ever produced.

Energetic and indefatigable, with an uncommonly clear perception, and endowed with a vigorous and powerful intellect wherever he might be, he was at once recognized as an individual of no ordinary ability. Wherever he has been associated with his fellow men, he has been an acknowledged leader.

For the early social and religious privileges which the citizens of this State enjoyed, they were to him largely indebted. He was early selected to represent both the towns in which he resided in the Legislature of Massachusetts, of which State we were then but a District. His activity and ability in that capacity was preeminently beneficial not only to his immediate constituency, but to the entire district.

Many important legislative enactments referring to Maine, were passed at his insistance. It is supposed that it was mainly owing to his influence that we were enabled to be separated from Massachusetts, and apply for admission into the Union as an independent State.

General King was the first governor of Maine, Commissioner of the Spanish Claims, Commissioner for the erection of the State House at Augusta, and for many years collector of customs for this port. He was a person who received high military distinction, and was First Grand Master of the Masonic Fraternity.

On page 2 of the same paper was an account of the funeral, which took place on Saturday, June 19:

Last Saturday was a day long to be remembered by the citizens of Bath. Early in the morning an observing person could have easily perceived that some event of no ordinary importance had occurred. Quiet demeanor, suppressed voices, and sorrowful countenances were noticeable throughout our usually active city.

Soon were to be seen the habiliments of mourning. Our country's flag, the cheering "Stars and Stripes" were clad with the sorrowful insignia which bespeaks public affliction.

It was fit that there should be general sorrow and public demonstration of grief. It was fit that our national banner should wear the garb of mourning when there was numbered with the dead one of those hardy heroes who has ever been so prompt and so proud to rally in support of its honor! Our citizens did honor to themselves no less than to the remains of the illustrious dead, by the public universal sorrow, at the final departure of one of our most distinguished citizens.

The public streets of the city were deeply dressed with mourning from early in the morning 'til night.

The funeral services at the late residence of the deceased were conducted by the Rev. Mr. Fisk.

After the funeral services were concluded the Masonic fraternity assumed the charge of the remains and a procession was formed in the following order, under the direction of R. R. Smith, chief marshal:

Bath Brass Band
Bath City Grays
Lincoln Lodge, Wiscasset
United Lodge, Brunswick
Richmond Lodge, Richmond
Solar Lodge, Bath
Grand Lodge of Maine
Remains of the deceased
Chief Mourners
Governor and Council
Mayor and President of the Common Council of Bath
Board of Aldermen
Common Council of Bath

The procession proceeded to Vine, Washington and North streets to the beautiful square in Maple Grove Cemetery which some years ago was reserved for the mournful purpose to which it has just been devoted.

Nothing can exceed the solemn grandeur of the Masonic ceremony at the grave of one of their brethren. Grief — deep, earnest, heartfelt, but not grief without hope, strong and abiding, in the glorious immortality of their deceased brother, was on that occasion manifested.

This peculiarly solemn and interesting part of the exercises was performed by Ex-Gov. Robert P. Dunlap of Brunswick, who is General Grand High Priest of the General Grand Chapter of the United States — assisted by Rev. Uriah Balkam, Grand Chaplain.

The dignified, and at the same time affectionate solemnity with which Ex-Gov. Dunlap performed his part of the services was highly creditable to himself, befitting the occasion, and worthy of the illustrious and beloved deceased.

In the performance of these last sad rites all concerned acted their parts in a manner highly appropriate.

The solemn dirgelike music of the band seemed to invoke the spirit of mourning; the tolling of bells and the solemn sound of minute guns broke the stillness of the air. The City Grays ever prompt with their presence can diffuse cheerfulness, or their services be beneficial; by their sad, although soldier-like appearance, gave evidence that they felt that they had escorted to the grave the remains of an elder soldier and a brother. Our citizens all appeared to feel that it was a time to mourn over the grave of the departed, a day when it was manliness to weep and be afflicted.[3]

Elsewhere in the paper there appeared a decree by the city government, which adopted resolutions on the death of Governor William King, and directed the Mayor to cause the bells to continue ringing from the departure to the return of the funeral procession.

Not long after the funeral, Ann moved to Portland to live with her son, taking only her personal possessions and a few articles of furniture she cherished. Asa Redington, in charge of the estate, had the furniture sold at auction. Mary Elizabeth's piano, among other things, was sold to Major Thomas Harward and taken to his home, later the Old Couples' Home at the north end of the city. Today it is in the Bath Marine Museum.

King's library was purchased by George F. and John Patten for $300, and by them presented to the Patten Library Association with the following letter:

> Having purchased the library, cases, maps and globes which were the property of Governor King, we present the same to the Patten Library Association of Bath, on the condition that the same revert

to the donors should the association be dissolved, and on further condition that a suitable room be procured for the whole library.

This library was accepted and today occupies a special bookcase in the main reading room of the Patten Free Library.

Soon after Ann left for Portland, the government sold the King house to Jeremiah Robinson. In 1853 it was moved to the corner of Front and Vine streets to a lot Robinson bought from the Kennebec and Portland Railroad. Jacob Leach bought it in 1859 and sold it to Jere Shannon in 1871. It was known as the Shannon House until Nelson L. Jackson bought it and renamed it King's Tavern in 1911. When it was taken down in 1926 to make way for the Vine Street approach to the Carlton Bridge, it was discovered that the original structure, built in 1800, had been a story and a half high. As a hotel, it ultimately reached the height of four stories above the basement.

The government built a customs house and post office on the lot vacated by the old mansion, and in 1859 the customs office in the old Bath Bank was moved to its new location and the bank sold to the Sagadahoc Bank. Today (1978) the customs house and post office have been moved to a new building on the corner of Washington Street and Leeman Highway.

Ann died in Portland, on July 4, 1857, and was buried in the family lot in Maple Grove Cemetery beside her husband and Mary Elizabeth. In addition to his father, mother, and Mary Elizabeth, Cyrus William and his wife Sarah are buried there. He died on April 16, 1881, aged sixty-three, and his wife Sarah, on July 31, 1895, aged seventy-one years, eleven months.

In 1853 the State Legislature passed a resolve, which was approved on March 31, appropriating $500 to be spent on raising a suitable monument on William King's grave in "Commemoration of his distinguished ability and sagacity as a statesman; and prominence and successful service in behalf of the interests of his native state." On March 27, 1897, the State Legislature made a further appropriation of $1,000 for remodeling the monument and putting it under perpetual care, the City of Bath receiving half of the $1,000 and agreeing to cause the object of the appropriation to be ever kept in sight of the trustees of the cemetery grounds.

GENERAL WILLIAM KING

Each side of the obelisk contains a medallion. The front side to the south represents the State, the westerly side is inscribed:

> Erected by
> The State of Maine
> To the memory of
> Its First Governor
> WILLIAM KING
> Who died July 17, 1852
> Aged 84 years

The Easterly side reads:

> Erected by
> The State in
> 1855
> Remodeled by
> The State in
> 1899

Why William King was chosen as the representative man of Maine, whose statue was her first contribution to the hall of sculptured heroes in the Capitol at Washington, D.C. was explained, according to Mrs. A. J. Swasey in her *Reminiscences of William King:* Very satisfactorily were these questions answered upon the occasion of the "unveiling" of the statue, in speeches by our Maine senators and representatives, and particularly well by the fine speech of Mr. Frye in the House, who showed by his faithful portrayal of Governor King's public career and character why he was a truly representative man of our State, and by his delicate touches upon his personal characteristics why his memory was to be held in honor by us all.

Mrs. Swasey adds a personal touch in her reaction to the statue:

> The noble statue by Simmons represents General King as a younger man than our memory calls up. It is not the grey-haired man, a little bent with age, who we used to see striding about the windy streets, with his blue cloak closely wrapped about him; or walking with stately steps up the aisle of the old North Church, with the cloak falling back from his shoulders, and displaying the scarlet lining, a touch of color in the somber meetinghouse

particularly attractive to us; but we know that it presents truthfully all the finer personal appearance of his more vigorous days, and as a work of art, we are proud to hear it pronounced the finest in the collection and to claim it as a representative of one of Maine's most honorable men, by one of Maine's most gifted sons.[4]

Appendices

I. William King's Merchant Fleet
II. Genealogical Material on the King Family from William's Generation On
III. Notes
IV. Bibliography

I. WILLIAM KING'S MERCHANT FLEET

Vessels King owned, or partly owned, or may have chartered or managed, mentioned in his letters and in other sources

What itemized information I could find on King's vessels came primarily from the Bath Marine Museum files, from such compilations as Henry Owen's list of vessels built in the Customs District in Bath, and his scrapbook of newspaper clippings; and the Preble and Partridge and Applebee lists.

Much of the material was also gleaned from William Baker's maritime history of Bath and environs; Fairburn's Merchant Sail; and other titles listed in the Bibliography; and from such documents at the Maine Historical Society Library as Leonard B. Chapman's *Deering News Notes;* Merton G. Henry's paper on William King; and William King's letters on file.

ADRASTUS
Ship rigged
86' x 25' x 12'5"
233 tons
Built 1794 in Topsham on the Kennebec
Description: billet head, square stern
Owners: William King, Dr. Benjamin Jones Porter and Robert Lapish
Masters: Samuel Jameson, 1794; Captain Lapish, 1798
Sold at auction, May 25, 1798

ALEXANDER
Ship rigged
89' 7" x 26'8" x 13'4"
275 tons
Built 1802 in Pittston, Me.

GENERAL WILLIAM KING

Description: billet head and square stern
Owners: John O. Page, John Ring of Hallowell, and William King of Bath, 1803-1809
Masters: John Ring, 1802; Calvin Ballard, 1809

ANDROSCOGGIN
Brig rigged
75'10" x 22'7" x 9'
135 tons
Built 1799 in Topsham, Maine, by Isaac Perkins
Description: billet head, square stern
Owners: William King, Benjamin Jones Porter, John Ryan, Joseph Berry, and Joseph Foster

On April 11, 1800, Dr. Porter wrote to King:

"On searching the Androscoggin she is found very rotten. . . " She was probably repaired and replanked, for among King's papers, dated August 9, 1800 is a list of officers and marines to go aboard her, with their descriptions:

James Peterson, master, age 29, complexion light, five ft. six, from Brunswick, born in Duxbury, U.S.A.
Nehamiah Harding age 20, complexion light, five ft. six, from Brunswick, born in Truro, U.S.A.
James Clark age 23, complexion light, five ft. 4¾, Lynn, born in Lynn, U.S.A.
Andrew Reed age 32, complexion light, five ft. 5¼, Boothbay, born in Boothbay, U.S.A.
Ribert Wiley age 32, complexion light, five ft. 8½, Boothbay, born in Boothbay
Joseph Dominick age 22, complexion black, five ft. 8½, Philadelphia, born in Philadelphia
John Coombs age 20, complexion light, five ft. 11, Brunswick, born in Bath
Time of Entry.   Harding, July 21
                   Clark, July 25
                   Reed, Aug. 9
                   Wiley, Aug. 9
                   Dominick Aug. 10
                   Coombs, Aug. 9

According to the papers the *Androscoggin* arrived in New Orleans in April 1802, with Nehemiah Harding, Captain. Peterson did not sign for the voyage.

ANN
Brig rigged
90' x 26'1" x 13'1"
266 tons
Built 1810 in Bath, Me., probably named for King's wife
Description: billet head and square stern
Owners: William King and John Bosworth
Masters: John Page, 1810; Richard King Porter, 1816

A letter, dated Aug. 17, 1816, shows that the *Ann* not only carried produce but immigrants as well. Richard King wrote to his Uncle that the *Ann* had arrived from Cork, Ireland, and he had been obliged "to enter bonds in your behalf, and in penal sum of $12,000 that on case any of the aliens who came on your brig should become a charge, either themselves or their children to the Corporation of the City of New York within two years you shall endemnity for same."

CLEOPATRA
Ship rigged

The only record found on this ship was a list of the owners: William King; McLellan, Stinson and Weld, 16,000; and the master in 1818, Captain Stinson.

CONFIDENCE
Ship rigged
95'9½" x 28'6" x 14'3"
336 tons
Built 1801 or 1802 in Bath, Me.
Description: billet head and square stern
Owners: William King and Dr. Benjamin Jones Porter
Master: Tristan Redman, 1802-03

A letter from Captain Tristan Redman tells of the fate of the *Confidence:*

> On the 26th of November (1802) at the mouth of the river (at Bordeaux) blowing heavy from westward, we made the light on the 25th at eight in the evening, kept her off until eight in the morning. Saw several boats coming out. We stood in with our signal for a pilot. No one coming to us we were obliged to keep the ship before the wind and sea. At ten o'clock we struck on a reef. At 12 the ship came to pieces. Nothing remained but the upper deck. We beat over the reef on that with the flood tide and the ebb taking us toward the reef. Several boats within sight of us, taking off the plunder, never came to take us off. We went near the reef again and taking the flood again and the wind shifting landed us on shore.

We lost Caleb Burbank in attempting to jump ashore, not knowing when to jump, it being very dark. The poor woman died, lashed on the deck, three hours before we got in. I have saved some of the rigging what sold for two thousand livres and part of the masts brought forty of them. We saved nothing of our clothes, only what we had on. The masts are not sold there is no demand for them at present. Mr. Lee has the managing of the business.

William Lee of Bordeaux did not fully trust the captain, sold sails, rigging, timber and spars, made about $4,000 to $5,000 on the sale and finally turned it over to Porter & King.

EAGLE
Schooner
Dimensions: not known
Where built: not known
Master: Captain Sprague at St. Kitts in 1790; Capt. Woodward, April 9, 1807.

(It is not clear who her owners were, but she is mentioned in articles by Henry Owen and Richard Hallet. In King's letters 1790-1801, Captain Lapish advises that she is too small for a run to Liverpool. A letter from Norfolk dated April 9, 1807, to King reads, "Your schooner, *Eagle*, Capt. Woodward, arrived here this day after a passage of 30 days." Earlier, on May 20, 1803, a letter from J. Andrews states, "You will receive 500 t. oakham by schooner *Eagle.*" King probably owned either part or all of her.)

ELEANOR
Brig rigged
Owner: William King
No other information.

FAIR AMERICAN
Ship rigged
79'6" x 23'6" x 11'6½"
186 tons
Built 1802 in Bath, Me., by Joshua Shaw
Description: billet head and square stern
Owners: William King and Robert Harding
Masters: John Spear, 1803; Capt. William Still, 1804; Robert Harding, 1807

FERDINAND
Brig rigged
77'11" x 23' x 10¼'
155 tons, as registered in the Bath Customs House

Built 1798 in Bath. On Dec. 11, 1799, repaired in Wiscasset; March 20, 1802, repaired, with new deck and quarter deck raised; insured for $5,000, February 24, 1803
Description: billet head, square stern
Owners: William King and Benjamin Jones Porter, 1798-1804
Masters: Robert Bosworth, mate Joseph Bosworth, 1799; James Jameson, 1801; Capt. Lane, 1804

Ran aground at Rye Beach, New Hampshire and was towed to Portsmouth and sold, December, 1804

FLORIDA
No information, except it was sold by William King to Mr. John Borden in lieu of 3300 pounds to settle a debt.

FRIENDSHIP
Schooner rigged
 No information, except that Capt. Robert Bosworth was master; and she sailed between Savannah and Boston, carrying cotton.

GANGES
Ship rigged
99'5" x 27'5" x 13'7"
329 tons
Built 1810 in Wiscasset
Description: billet head and square stern
Owners: Thomas Nichols; transferred to William King, July 28, 1818
Masters: Prince Baxter (?); Samuel Peterson, 1812

GUARDIAN
Schooner rigged
68'8" x 23'6" x 9'2"
124 tons
Built 1795 in Brunswick
Description: billet head and square stern
Owners: William King, Benjamin Jones Porter of Topsham, and Sylvanus Cushman, of Brunswick, 1795 (according to Bath Records); William King, Benjamin Jones Porter and William Cushman, Merchants, Topsham (according to Portland & Falmouth Records)
Masters: Hezikiah Harding, Tristam Redman, 1798

> Captain Redman left hardwood plank, the property of Captain Acton Patten, with Captain Nathaniel Curtis in the south end of Boston in 1798, which he was later requested to remove.

GENERAL WILLIAM KING

HARMONY
Brig rigged
88'7" x 25' x 10½'
194 tons
Built 1808 or 1809
Master builder: George Skolfield in Topsham
Owner: William King
Masters: John Skolfield, 1809; Capt. Melcher, 1810

HENRY
Brig rigged
190 or 191 tons
Built 1811
Master builder: John Henry in Bowdoinham, Me.
Owners: Isaiah Crooker, 1814; that year William King bought one-half interest for $2,000.

> Note: An article on page 12 of Henry Owen's Scrapbook at the Bath Marine Museum notes the finding of a ledger (1806-1815) of Elijah Low & Co., in which William King is mentioned as the owner of the *Henry*. King paid 75 percent on bills for the brig in September 1818.

HOMER
Ship rigged
Owners: Dr. Benjamin Porter; in 1818, three-fourths of his ownership transferred to William King to offset losses he incurred on Porter's behalf.
Master: Robert McKown

HURON
Brig rigged
83'6" x 23'10½" x 10'
173 or 174 tons
Built 1806 by Thomas Lombard at Bath
Description: billet head and square stern
Owners: William King and Thomas Lombard, Bath, 1807
Masters: Richard K. Porter, 1807; Captain Foote, 1811; Capt. Martin to Baltimore, April, 1818; Captain Mathews, 1818

INDUSTRY
Sloop rigged
No other information obtained.

MARGARETTE or MARGARETTA
Brig rigged
77'9" x 23' x 11'6"
178 tons
Built 1813 in Newburyport, Mass.
Description: no figurehead, square stern
Owner: William King purchased one-half interest in the brig, Oct. 7, 1813 for $1775.
Master: Capt. Kobs, 1814

Note: This vessel served to bring the *Boxer* and *Enterprise* together, resulting in a victory for the American vessel at a terrible cost to both sides. This brig may have been the former *Latonia* or one of about the same size and name.

A letter from G. Deblois relates her "capture off the Bar. Her trial was set next Monday 7th inst at the Admiralty Court, Savannah." He expected her to be condemned there.

From Captain Kobs: "Heard from Savannah that the brig and cargo, 11 pinchons of rum might have been bonded," but Mr. Charlton, his lawyer, advised him not to do so at present... "By the next mail I hope to have it in my power to say that the vessel is cleared and suffered to go to port to which she was bound, Amelia, from whence, the only place she can go to will be Havana in ballast."

MINERVA
Schooner rigged
70' x 20'10" x 7'6"
Built 1795 in Brunswick
Owners: William King and Benjamin Jones Porter of Topsham in 1793; James Tisdale, Boston; and Peleg Tallman, Bath, in 1795
Masters: John Minott, 1793; Nathaniel Melcher (Preble and Partridge List)

NANCY
Brig rigged
78' x 23'6" x 11'9"
178 or 179 tons
Built 1793 in Brunswick
Owners: William King, Benjamin Jones Porter, and John Richardson, 1800
Masters: John Dunlap, Andrew Dunning, John Lane, and Captain Martin

The *Nancy* was captured by the British man-o-war *Hornet* on suspicion of having infringed the revenue laws and was brought into Montserrat. King protested the action and the British let her go free.

GENERAL WILLIAM KING

John Lane was long in the employ of William King, but he finally, on a bribery fee of $40.00 caused King much trouble.

A note among King's papers from his agent reads: "Before me is a clearance paper of the schooner, *NANCY*, dated at Berbric, Oct. 4, in the 40th year of His Magesty's reign, which shows she was 106 tons burthen, mounted no guns and navigated with 4 men, 1800 goods to the amount of 96 pounds (English money) was the equal of 233 Spanish dollars and 22 cents."

NEPTUNE
Brig rigged
Master: Captain Bubbidge.

No information except that she did some business for William King in 1805.

NYMPH
Brig rigged

No information other than concerning her capture by a Spanish privateer as related in the text.

ORANGE
Schooner rigged
Built by James Andrews and John Anderson
Dimensions: not known
Weight: not known
Owners: Wades & Clopper, Boston, Mass. 1802.
Masters: Captain Philips, 1802; Captains Holman and Saunders.

A note to King as manager of the schooner reads: "We take the liberty to hand you a bill of sale for 1/3 and request you will have the names of Edw. Blake Jr. and Nath. Ruddell Sturgis put on the Register. When you take it out for Schooner one third — We understand she is to be called John and James. We wil thank you to let us know the probable time she will be ready to take her cargo — Blake and Sturgis."

OSIRIS
Ship rigged
81'9" x 11'9"
198 tons
Built 1796 in Topsham
Description: billet head and square stern
Owners: William King and Benjamin Jones Porter, 1796
Masters: William King, 1796; Thomas Farnam, 1797; Tristam Redman, 1799, and John Lane mate.

PERSERVERANCE
Brig rigged
87'4" x 24'9½" x 12'4¾"
235 tons
Built 1808 in Bath by John Bosworth
Description: billet head and square stern
Owner: William King, sole owner
Master: John Page, 1808

RAINBOW
No information except that Joseph Boyd, King's brother-in-law, bought a half-interest in her in April, 1807. King had shares in her and had a bill of sale for her and may have had charge of her from the Boston office, in May, 1818.

REBECCA
Schooner rigged
Built in Freeport, 1795
No other information except that she was either chartered or owned at one time by King.

RESERVE
Ship rigged
101'7" x 30' x 15'
395 tons
Built 1804 or 1805 in Bath by John Bosworth
Description: billet head omitted; she had a figurehead and a square stern
Owner: William King
Masters: Tristan Redman, 1805; Matthew Prior, 1805; Capt, Rich, 1819

RESOLUTION
Ship rigged
100'3" x 28'4" x 14'2"
353 tons
Built 1807 in Bath by John Bosworth
Description: billet head and square stern
Owner: William King
Masters: Robert McKown, 1809-1815; Capt. Wm. Haddean, 1818-1819

From a letter dated Jan. 2, 1811, from Capt. McKown in Savannah, Ga., it appears that the ship, *United States* was at the port loading with lumber for Liverpool. McKown stated, "The demand for lumber is the greatest I ever saw. The *Resolution* is here throwing out ballast, six men have

GENERAL WILLIAM KING

deserted and the great number of ships here makes seamen scarce. The timber is ready for her to begin on.

"The *Reserve* is here and taking on a load of cotton, but as laborers are scarce only our crew can be worked."

At Bermuda, Mar. 5, 1811, King received this letter from Capt. McKown:

Gen. King,

Sir, I have to inform you that we had the misfortune to spring a leak on the 27th of February last Lat. 34° 27" and Long. 71° 36". We could not free her with both pumps. We cleared her decks but the leak still continued. On the 1st of March we began to clear her between the decks, as we thought she would fill and the cotton would blow up her deck. We got out about 100 bags of cotton, and on the 2nd of March came to anchor on the east end of the island and got eight hands to pump on the 3d and 4th. We had a heavy gale of wind which we rode out with both anchors ahead. This day we have got into the safety port of the town of St. George. If it is possible to find the leak without unloading, we will get from here as soon as possible. If we have to unload here, God only knows when we shall get off from here. We have as much as we can do with eight hands besides our own men to keep her up. If we had not gotten her here the day we did, we should have filled as the water had gained about 3½ feet with both pumps going all the time as hard as we could work them.

I remain Sir you Humble Svt., Rob. McKown

Capt. McKown must have been able to locate and repair the leak, for a letter written to William, from his nephew, James Gore King, dated at New York, Aug. 9, 1815, informs his uncle that his ship *Resolution* sailed on that day for Bath and one article on board of her, "is $2000 in silver in a keg." This was part of the receipts from the sale of sugar in New York amounting to some $5000; the rest was held subject to William King's order.

A bill of lading signed at Savannah, Ga., by Capt. Robert McKown, May 10, 1810, shows what was on a load for the good ship *Resolution* at that time and place as follows:

302 pitchpine logs
241 boards and plank
22,287 hogshead stoves
1,907 headings
23 m 500 reeds for the acct and risk of Mr. Wm. King, a native citizen of the U.S.A. for Liverpool, Eng.

REUNION
Ship rigged
92' x 26'5" x 13'3"

281 tons
Built 1800 in Bath
Description: billet head and square stern
Owners: William King and Benjamin Jones Porter, 1801
Masters: Tristam Redman, 1801; James Bond, 1803; David Bond, 1804; Capt. Thomas, Capt. James Sampson, 1805; Capt. Haddean, 1818

> Note: The *Reunion* paid her cost three times over when first put into service.

TYPHYS
Ship rigged
Owners: Seven-eighths of this vessel became King's as repayment for a loan to Dr. Benjamin Porter.
Master: Captain Ezekiel Purington

> No other information except that given in text.

UNITED STATES
Ship rigged
96' x 26'9" x 13'4½"
301 tons

Built 1803 in Woolwich, Me.
Description: billet head and square stern
Owners: William King of Bath and Samuel Reed of Woolwich, 1803-1811
Masters: Capt. Samuel Reed, 1803; Capt. James Oliver, 1809; Richard King Porter, 1810.

> Note: In November 1803, Captain Reed wrote to King: "The ship *United States* is just right for Liverpool trade from Savannah. She is the best ship that I ever sailed in. She sails very fast and works well."

VALARIUS
Brig rigged
78' x 22'8½" x 8'11"
137 tons
Built 1801 in Bath
Description: billet head and square stern
Owners: William King, James Small, and Benjamin Jones Porter of Topsham
Masters: Robert Harding, 1801-1802; James Oliver, April 1802; Capt. Gross, 1806

> Note: She had one mate and six seamen for crew.

VIGILANT
Ship rigged

GENERAL WILLIAM KING

99'8" x 28'1" x 11'2"
210 tons
Built 1806 at Bath by John Bosworth
Description: billed head and square stern
Owners: Robert Bosworth and William King
Masters: Robert Bosworth, 1806; Jos. Coombs, 1809

"Statement of the value of the Ship *Vigilent* 364 tons burthen on her second Voyage owned by William King — also of her freight and premium of Insurance on Ship and freight at the time of her sailing from Virginia to the North of Europe in December 1809 and the sums advanced Capt. Coombs the Master by Logan Lenox Company and Lodges & Tooth Merchants of Liverpool to enable the Captain to obtain the release of the Ship (taken by French privateer *Prince of Callis*, Capt. Glasson, in the North Sea, carried to the Isle of Terschilling where her cargo was removed, and put on shore) to pay expenses.

Ship Vigilent valued at		$15,000.00
Freight on 442 Hds Tobacco at 4.10	1989. 0. 0	
Freight on 56 Bales Cotton	137. 4. 0	
Five pr. ct passage on the above	106. 6. 2	
	2032 10 2	
Prem. of Insurance on above Dols.		9,914.80
		24,914.80
December 1809 to North of Europe		1,744.58
To this Sum advanced Capt. Coombs by		
Logan Lenox & Company of Liverpool	400. 0. 0	
To this Sum advanced Coombs by		
Lodges & Tooth of Liverpool	800. 0. 0	
	1200 pounds	5,333.32
		31,997.50'"*

*Copied at the Bath Marine Museum, from William Torrey, *Notorial Records* (Vol. 6), June 1835. Captain Coombs got the ship off and finally to New Orleans, July 12, 1812, in serious need of repair.

VISITOR

Brig rigged
85'8" x 25'3" x 11'2"
Built 1815 in Bath by Peleg Sprague
Description: billet head and square stern
Owners: William King, Peter H. Green of Bath, and Clement Martin of Harpswell, 1815-1819
Masters: Clement Martin, Charles Thomas, 1819

VOLANT
Ship rigged
Owner: William King
    No other information

VOLUNTEER
Brig rigged
Dimensions: not known
Built 1800 or 1801 in Bath
Owners: Porter & King, James Andrews
Master: Robert Bosworth, 1801

    Note: In 1802 Capt. Robert Bosworth failed to sell the *Volunteer* in Holland and came home empty. She sailed to Liverpool from Savannah with cotton in 28 days in Mar. 1803, insured for $3000.

    July 23, 1803, James Andrews went to Philadelphia and sold the *Volunteer* for $7500 for King. He had contracted to sell her with Mr. Winthrop in Boston, Mar. 3, 1803.

II. GENEALOGICAL NOTES ON THE KING FAMILY FROM WILLIAM KING'S GENERATION ON

1. The Rufus King Family of New York*

RUFUS KING,[1] born at Scarborough, Maine, March 24, 1755, to Richard and Isabella (Bragdon) King, was graduated at Harvard in 1777. He enlisted in the Continental army during the next year and was assigned as aide-de-camp to General John Sullivan in the Rhode Island campaign. In 1778, he established his residence in Newbury, Massachusetts, and studied law under Theophilus Parsons, chief justice of the Commonwealth. Two years later, he was admitted to the bar and became a popular legal practitioner in the Bay State. After serving a single year in the Massachusetts General Court, he was chosen its representative to the Continental Congress, and while acting in the latter capacity he became prominent as the advocate to prohibit the extension of slavery throughout the colonies.

Rufus was a leading member of the Constitutional Convention of 1787 and returned to Massachusetts to work for ratification of the constitution by that state.

On March 30, 1786, he married Mary, b. Oct. 17, 1769, dau. of John Alsop, a wealthy merchant of New York who had represented that district in the Continental Congress. Having moved to New York, Rufus King became Federalist U.S. Senator from that state, from 1789 to 1796. He was minister to London from 1796 to 1803, and served again in the Senate from 1813 to 1825. In 1816 he was an unsuccessful candidate for governor, and that same year received thirty-four electoral votes for President, having been the Federalist candidate for Vice-President in 1804 and 1808. His last service was again at the Court of London in 1825-26. His health failing, he returned to this country and died at his home on Long Island (N.Y.) on April 26, 1827.

*Information gathered from *Maine Historical and Genealogical Recorder,* Wm. H. Smith, "The King Family of New York," Vol. I, No. 4 (1884), Portland, Me.: S. M. Watson, Publisher, pp. 182-86.

The children of Rufus and Mary King were:

John Alsop,[2] b. Jan. 3, 1788; d. July 8, 1867. He became secretary of the American Legation at London in 1825; was a member of the U.S. Congress from the State of New York, 1849-51; governor of New York, 1856 and 1858. He m. Jan. 3, 1810, Mary, b. 1790, dau. of Cornelius and Elizabeth Ray. Their children were:

Mary,[3] b. Oct. 29, 1810; m. P. M. Nightingale, of Cumberland Island, Georgia, grandson of General Greene of the Continental Army. Their children:

    Louisa Greene[4]
    Mary Ray,[4] m. Dr. Robert Troup, of Georgia
    Martha[4]
    John Alsop King,[4] m. Mary Heyward Troup
    Ellen,[4] m. Henry M. Fuller
    Elizabeth[4]
    William,[4] m. Ellen D. Hazlehurst

Charles Ray,[3] b. Mar. 16, 1813; m. 1st, Hannah Fisher, of Philadelphia. Their children:

    Mary Fisher,[4] m. Charles Denney
    John Alsop[4]

M. 2nd, Nancy Fisher, sister of first wife.

Elizabeth Ray,[3] b. Aug., 1815; m. Aug., 1833, Henry Van Rensselaer, General U.S. Army, son of Stephen Van Rensselaer, Patroon of Albany. Their children:

    Mary,[4] m. John H. Screven, of South Carolina
    Cornelia,[4] m. James L. Kennedy, of New York; had a son,
        Van Rensselaer Kennedy[5]
    Stephen,[4] m. Matilda C. Heckscher
    Euphemia[4]
    Elizabeth,[4] m. Geo. Waddington
    John King,[4] m. May D. King, dau. of A. Gracie King
    Katherine,[4] m. Francis Delafield, M.D.
    Henry[4]

John,[3] b. July 14, 1817; New York State Senator, 1874-75; m. Mary Cobden, dau. of Philip Rhinelander. Their children:

    Mary Rhinelander[4]
    Cornelia[4]
    Alice[4]
    Frederica[4]
    Ellen[4]

Caroline,[3] b. June 1, 1820; m. Jas. Gore King jr., Sept. 7, 1843. (See children under record of J. G. King jr.)

Richard,[3] birth date not found; m. Elizabeth Lewis, of Philadelphia, Sept., 1847. Their children:

    John,[4] and Lewis,[4] twins
    Elizabeth[4]

GENERAL WILLIAM KING 161

Richard,[4] m. Isabel Chater
Cornelia,[3] b. Mar. 31, 1824
Charles,[2] b. Mar. 16, 1789; date of death not found. He served through two campaigns of the War of 1812; was elected a member of the legislature of the State of New York in 1813. Later, he became president of Columbia College, New York; m. 1st, Eliza Gracie, Mar. 16, 1810. Their children:
Eliza Gracie,[3] m. Rev. Charles H. Halsey. Their children:
Eliza Gracie,[4] m. Charles Suydam
Emily,[4] m. Frederick Vincent
Hetty,[4] m. Otis Pinneo, M.D.
Charles[4]
William Frederick,[4] m. Annie Brewster
Hetty,[3] m. John G. Martin, of Asheville, N.C.
Rufus,[3] m. 1st, Ellen Elliott, of Albany; 2nd, Susan, sister of first wife. Their children:
Charles,[4] m. Miss York
Fanny,[4] m. Edmund A. Ward
William Gracie,[3] m. Adeline McKee. Their children:
Rufus,[4] m. Miss Williamson, gr. dau. of Chancellor Williamson of N.J.
Mary,[4] m. Charles Clark
Eliza Gracie,[4] m. Beverly Robinson jr.
Charles,[3] no dates.
Alice Consett,[3] m. Rev. Andrew Bell Paterson. Their children:
Alice,[4] m. Charles Mann
Henrietta,[4] m. _____, Officer
Cornelia Bell[4]
Eliza Gracie,[4] m. Richard Bond
Emily Sophia,[4] d. young
Archibald Gracie,[3] d. young
Emily Sophia,[3] m. Dec. 1852, Stephen Van Rensselaer Paterson; d. April 4, 1853.
Charles,[2] m. 2nd, Henrietta, dau. of Cornelius Low, of N.Y. Their children:
Anne Johnson[3]
Cornelius Low,[3] m. 1st, Julia Lawrence; 2nd, Janet DeKay
Henrietta Low[3]
Gertrude Wallace,[3] m. Eugene Schuyler, U.S. Minister to Greece
Mary Alsop,[3] m. Mr. Waddington, Minister Foreign Affairs, France
Augustus Fleming,[3] d. young
James Gore,[2] b. May 8, 1791; member of Congress from the State of New Jersey, 1849-51; head of the banking house of Jas. G. King's Sons; m. Feb. 4, 1813, Sarah Rogers, b. Dec. 14, 1791, dau. of Archibald Gracie, and gt. gr. dau. of Thomas Fitch, last colonial governor of Connecticut. Their children:
Caroline,[3] b. Nov. 10, 1813; m. May 8, 1837, Denning Duer, son of Judge Wm. A. Duer, president of Columbia College, N.Y., gr. grandson of

William Alexander Lord Sterling, Brig.-Gen. of the Continental Army. Their children:

    Sarah Gracie,[4] b. Oct. 2, 1838.

    Edward Alexander,[4] b. Mar. 14, 1840; m. Anna, dau. of John Van Buren, gr. dau. of Martin Van Buren, President of the U.S.A.

    James Gore King,[4] b. Sept. 9, 1841; m. Elizabeth Meads, of Albany

    Rufus King,[4] b. July 26, 1843; d. unm.

    Amy Maria,[4] b. May 20, 1845

    William Alexander,[4] b. Nov. 23, 1849; m. Ellen Travers

    Denning,[4] b. Sept. 15, 1850; m. Louise Suydam

Sarah Gracie,[3] b. Aug. 8, 1815; d. Oct., 1815

Harriet,[3] b. June 2, 1817; m. May 19, 1836, George Wilkes, M.D. Their children:

    Grace,[4] b. Mar. 27, 1837

    Harriet King,[4] b. April 9, 1838

James,[3] b. May 3, 1819; Judge of the Supreme Court, State of N.Y., 1851; afterward partner in the banking house of Jas. G. King's Sons; m. Caroline King, dau. of John A. King, Sept. 7, 1843. Their children:

    James,[4] b. June 17, 1844; d. July 29, 1862

    John Alsop,[4] b. Aug. 15, 1846; m. 1874, Elizabeth W. Tompkins

    Mary Ray,[4] b. Dec. 26, 1848; m. 1871, Benj. Franklin Lee

    Harriet,[4] b. Oct. 15, 1851; d. Feb. 13, 1873

    Caroline,[4] b. June 1, 1854; d. Oct. 21, 1854

Archibald Gracie,[3] b. July 11, 1821; treasurer 1865-73, and subsequently president, of the Institution for Savings of Merchants' Clerks, headquarters of the banking house of Jas. G. King's Sons, from May 1873 to May 1881, and trustee from 1861 to 1881; m. May 8, 1845, Elizabeth D., dau. of Wm. A. Duer, gt. gr. dau. of William Alexander Lord Sterling. Their children:

    May,[4] b. May 25, 1848; m. Oct. 4, 1871, John King Van Rensselaer, grandson of Patroon of Albany

    Sarah Gracie,[4] b. Oct. 5, 1850; m. Dec. 1, 1875, Frederick Bronson, of Verna Greenfield Hill, Conn., grandson of Isaac Bronson, first president of the Bridgeport Bank

    Frederick Gore,[4] b. Oct. 25, 1852; m. Jessie Arklay, gt. gr. dau. of Bishop Parker, Episcopal of Mass.

Henry Myers,[3] b. Sept. 15, 1824; d. Aug. 9, 1825

Mary,[3] b. June 31, 1826; m. Nov. 12, 1856, Edgar H. Richards. Their children:

    Edgar,[4] b. Feb. 23, 1858

    James Gore King,[4] b. May 15, 1859

    Frederick Gore,[4] b. May 3, 1863

    Gracie,[4] b. Dec. 25, 1867

Frederica Gore,[3] b. July 2, 1829; m. Nov. 19, 1857, John Chandler Bancroft Davis (eldest son of John Davis, U.S. Senator from Mass., 1835-53); secretary of the American Legation, London, 1849-53; assistant Secretary of State, 1869-71,

GENERAL WILLIAM KING 163

73-74, 81-82; agent of the U.S. at Geneva (Alabama claims), 1872; envoy to Germany, 1874-77; judge of the Court of Claims, 1877-81; 1883.

Edward,[3] b. July 30, 1833; president of the Union Trust Co. of N.Y.; m. Isabella Ramsey Cochrane. Their children:
  Isabella[4]
  Alice[4]
  James[4]
  Elizabeth[4]
  Rupert[4]

Fanny,[3] b. July 8, 1836; m. Nov. 15, 1859, James Latimer McLane, b. Sept. 2, 1834, son of Louis McLane, Secretary of State, 1833, grandson of Allan McLane, captain in the Continental Army. Their children:
  Katherine Milligan,[4] b. Sept.15, 1860
  James Gore King,[4] b. Feb. 21, 1863; d. Dec. 20, 1867
  Allan,[4] b. Dec. 8, 1864
  Robert Milligan,[4] b. Nov. 30, 1867
  Fanny King,[4] b. Oct. 12, 1869
  Ethel,[4] b. Jan. 17, 1872; d. July 11, 1872
  Frederica Gore,[4] b. Sept. 2, 1877
  James Latimer,[4] b. July 20, 1879

Henry,[2] d. young.

Edward,[2] b. Mar. 13, 1795; d. at Cincinnati, Ohio, in 1831. He m. Sarah, dau. of Thomas Worthington, Governor of Ohio and president of the Ohio Senate.* Their children:
  Rufus,[3] m. Miss Reeves, of Cincinnati
  Thomas Worthingon[3]

Frederick Gore,[2] b. Feb. 6, 1802; m. Emily Post. No issue.

Caroline,[2] b. Nov. 10, 1813; d. young.

II. The Southgate Family of Scarborough*

MARY, called by her friends "pretty Polly King," eldest daughter of Richard and Isabella (Bragdon) King, b. 1757; d. Mar. 30, 1824; m. Dr. Robert Southgate on June 23, 1773.

Robert Southgate, b. in Leicester, Mass., Oct. 26, 1741, moved to Scarborough in 1771; d. Nov. 2, 1823, aged 93. He was a physician whose talents and character soon won him a good position. Having some knowledge of law, he was appointed a

---

*In *Maine . . . Recorder* (Vol. I, No. 2), *op. cit.* Wm. M. Smith, in his article "The King Family of Maine" (pp. 33-40), reports that Edward was said to have been the cleverest son of Rufus King, and a most eloquent speaker.

judge in the Court of Common Sessions. He and his wife lived first on the southwest side of the Dunstan Landing road, where elms marked the location halfway to the corner, according to Augustus F. Moulton*. In 1805 Dr. Southgate built the big brick house on the northwest side of the Portland turnpike road, occupied later by his son, Judge Horatio Southgate. Through his marriage, Dr. Southgate acquired a large part of the King lands.

The children of Mary and Robert Southgate were:
> Mary King,² b. Sept. 4, 1775; d. June 22, 1795
> A daughter,² b. Jan. 9, 1777; d. same day
> A son,² b. Nov. 7, 1777; died the same day
> Isabella,² b. Mar. 29, 1779; m. Joseph C. Boyd of Portland, first treasurer of the State of Maine; d. early, leaving fifteen children.**

Augusta,³ the youngest, b. Jan. 10, 1819, m. Gen. Lloyd Tilghman.

Horatio,² b. Aug. 9, 1781, became judge and register of Probate Court; d. around 1864. His son, Horatio³ (no dates) was a bishop of the Episcopal Church.

Betsy,² also known as Betsey, Elizabeth or Elise, b. Sept. 24, 1783; m. 1803 to Walter Bowne, of Flushing, N.Y., who became the author of *A Girl's Life Eighty Years Ago,** composed mostly of letters written by his wife, who d. Feb. 19, 1809. Their children were:
> Walter,³ b. 1805
> Mary,³ b. July 1808

Octavia,² b. Sept. 13, 1786
Miranda,² b. Feb. 15, 1789; d. July 17, 1816
Frederick,² b. Aug. 9, 1791; d. May 29, 1813
Robert,² b. Oct. 14, 1796; d. July 6, 1799
Mary King,² b. 1799; m. Grenville Mellen; d. May 13, 1829

---

*Gleaned from original town records, copied by S. M. Watson and published in the *Maine . . . Recorder, op. cit.* (VI, 3), 1889, p. 397; and from A. F. Moulton, *Grandfather Tales of Scarborough* (Augusta, Me.: Katahdin Publishing Co., 1925), p. 71.

**A note in the *Recorder, op cit.* (II, 1), 1885, pp. 59-60 (signed E.B.L.), quotes from an address delivered Sept. 4, 1884, on the occasion of the Centenary of the Leicester Academy, by the Hon. William H. Rice, who gave an extract from an address delivered in 1847 by the Rev. Dr. Pierce of Brookline, Mass., who had been an assistant professor at the Academy: "Miss Isabella Southgate, from Scarborough, Maine, was a youth of transcendent beauty and accomplishments. Though in my class which I instructed at the Univesity were Dr. Channing, Judge Story, and other respectable scholars, yet I have never known one, male or female, of a more extraordinary mind than was evinced by that gifted young lady." E.B.L. goes on to say that the descendants of Isabella Southgate Boyd "remaining among us in 1885 are Col. Charles B. Merrill, Dr. John C. Merrill, Miss Mary Merrill and J. Hall Boyd, who are her grandchildren."

*New York: Scribners, 1888.

III. The Aaron Porter Family

PAULINA, youngest child of Richard and Isabella (Bragdon) King, was b. Mar. 1, 1759, at Dunstan Landing, Scarborough; m. Dr. Aaron Porter, of Biddeford, May 3, 1777. He was b. in Boxford, Mass., Mar. 28, 1752, the son of Moses Porter; studied medicine with Dr. Thomas Kittridge of Andover, Mass., settled in Biddeford in 1773, where in 1776 he became a town commissioner to procure gunpowder. In 1779 he bought 41 acres on the road leading to Buxton, but he did not live there. Instead, he built a two-story residence in the more thickly settled part of the town, on the road to Winter Harbor. He added a third story in 1800.

He was granted a township in Oxford County and the town of Porter was named for him. With two other persons, Jeremiah Hill and Matthew Cobb, he purchased a small lot of land in Saco, and erected a house there suitable for an academy. "A subscription paper" was circulated in an effort to gain money for the establishment of an academy. The builders also hinted at asking the State Legislature for aid. But it was not until later that the Saco Academy did occupy the building.

Dr. Porter sold his house on the road to Winter Harbor in 1810 and moved to Portland, where he lived first in a house on Federal Street; then had a three-story house built on Free Street (the southeast side of Free and next lot, easterly of Center Street), where his son Captain Richard Porter succeeded him. Aaron Porter d. June 30, 1837.

The children of Paulina and Aaron Porter were:

Rufus K.,[2] b. June 14, 1778; d. July 9, 1790, age 12

Moses,[2] b. Sept. 26, 1780; graduated from Harvard in 1802; d. June 1802, of yellow fever in an epidemic that hit Biddeford.

Mary,[2] b. Aug. 19, 1782; m. Nathaniel Coffin. They lived in Wiscasset, and William King and his wife were frequent visitors. Their house, according to *Sprague's Journal of Maine History,*[*] was called "Match Cottage," because a number of young ladies met their future husbands there, among them Rev. Edward Beecher, who met Isabella Jones, Mary Coffin's niece.

Richard K.,[2] b. July 20, 1784, in Biddeford; m. Polly or Mary Clapp, b. Sept. 25, 1788, dau. of Abigail (Partridge) and Elkanah Clapp, of Marshfield, Mass.; d. June 15, 1847. Richard was in command of his uncle William King's brig *Huron* in 1806, and ship *United States* in 1811. It was said that he made repairs on both when in

---

[*]Vol. 13, p. 20.

foreign countries that his uncle would not do in this country and thereby vexed King on account of the expense.

In 1827 Captain Porter resided in what was once the office building of Samuel Freeman Esq., on Middle St. in Portland. For a period of several years he was in the employ of the Pattens of Bath as a sailing master. He d. July 25, 1859, at his Mitchell Hill residence in Deering.

Richard and Mary had four daughters:

Elizabeth Clapp,[3] the youngest, m. Alexander W. Longfellow, brother of the poet.

Paulina,[2] b. May 26, 1786, m. Enoch Jones, a merchant of Bath. Their children were:

Isabella,[3] m. Edward Beecher, a brother of Harriet Beecher (Stowe).

Another daughter,[3] m. Ammi R. Mitchell, a merchant of Bath, July 22, 1817.

Isabella Bragdon,[2] b. April 25, 1788, m. Henry Homes, a Boston merchant, Sept. 20, 1814. Their children were:

William B.,[3] graduated from Illinois College

Francis,[3] graduated from Amherst College

Harriet,[2] b. April 25, 1790, m. Rev. Lyman Beecher, Oct. 29, 1817. She was his second wife and stepmother of Harriet Beecher (Stowe). It was said in a pen picture of Harriet that she had blue eyes, soft auburn hair, bound round with a black velvet ribbon "bandeau," and that she was particularly dainty and neat in all her ways. Her voice was sweet and her ways of moving and speaking graceful; "with hands partaking of pearl in appearance ornamented with finger rings."

They had three sons and a daughter. Harriet d. July 6, 1835.

A year later, Lyman married again, the third time.*

Almira,[2] b. Jan. 7, 1792; m. John Heath Goddard, of Portsmouth, N.H., Jan. 27, 1812

Rufus K.,[2] b. 1794; m. 1st, Emma E. Cooper and 2nd, Lucy Lee Hedge

Lucy,[2] and Elizabeth,[2] twins, b. Sept. 9, 1795; d. 1795

Lucy Elizabeth,[2] b. Aug. 26, 1797; m. John P. Brace, Nov. 1819

IV. The Richard King Jr. Family

RICHARD KING JR. was the oldest son of Richard and Mary (Black) King; b. Dec. 22, 1762; d. Oct. 27, 1830. According to A. F. Moulton, he lived on "Scottow Hill and was chiefly known for his peculiarities, and often referred to as

---

*Taken from "Notes on the King Family of Scarboro," by Leonard B. Chapman, published in the *Deering News* from the week of Feb. 20-22, through May 31, 1902, and included in the Scarborough Scrapbook of Nathan Goold, at the Maine Historical Society Library, Portland.

'Old Dick King.' "* A large-framed and witty man, he stayed in Scarborough all his life, farmed and built small sailing vessels. He was buried in the field a few rods from his house with his wife and some of his children. He m. Hannah Larrabee, Jan. 14, 1790, who d. in 1845. Their children were:

Cyrus,[2] b. May 4, 1790; m. Hannah Carter
Mary,[2] b. Oct. 12, 1791; d. young
William,[2] b. Jan. 18, 1793. Left home at the age of eighteen and never heard from again.
Eliza,[2] b. Sept. 30, 1796; m. Wm. Austin, of Windham, Me.**
Joseph Leland,[2] no birth date found; d. unm., 1815, in Windham
Robert Southgate,[2] b. Jan. 1, 1803; d. young
Benj. Sam'l Black,[2] b. 1803
Jane Ann,[2] b. Mar. 9, 1805; d. 1811
Hannah (Fidelia) Larrabee,[2] b. Jan. 9, 1808; m. Aaron Hawkes of Windham; as a widow lived with the youngest daughter, Mary E. Hawkes; had a granddaughter, Ina Lord McDavitt, who lived in Vineland, New Jersey, and in 1902 vouched for the above list of Richard's children.
Robert Southgate,[2] b. Mar. 14, 1811. Went West; m. Mercy Salmon, who d. in 1858, leaving eight children.
Mirander S.,[2] b. Aug. 9, 1813; m. Philip Gammon and lived in Windham and Naples; d. Oct. 7, 1854, in Falmouth.

The above list was also vouched for by Miss Mary Larrabee Whitney, age 89, of Burnham, Maine.

V. The Leland Family

ISABELLA, dau. of Richard and Mary (Black) King, b. Sept. 8, 1764; d. Sept. 12, 1770.

DORCAS, b. May 20, 1766; m. Joseph Leland, Dec. 28, 1786. They lived at Dunstan's Landing at first. Their children were:

Cyrus,[2] b. at the Landing, Sept. 27, 1787
Sarah,[2] b. at Phillipsburg (Hollis), Dec. 21, 1789; m. 1st Abel Boynton; 2nd, Hon. Edward Parker.
Elizabeth,[2] b. Nov. 29, 1791; m. Nathan Lord
Mary S.,[2] b. 1794; m. Frederick B. French

---

*Grandfather Tales of Scarborough, op. cit., p. 69.
**Maine... Recorder, op. cit., Vol. I, No. 1 (1884), p. 8, lists only these four children by name. The other children's names and information about them were provided from notes of Dorothy Robie Ashby, of Belmont, Mass.

Harriet,[2] b. Sept. 12, 1795; m. William Richardson of Bath, a descendant of Thomas Richardson, who settled in Woburn, Mass., in 1635. They had nine boys and one girl. They lived in Bath and it was William who took the mortgage on William King's house and land in bath.* When William King died, William Richardson was also dead. The heirs signing off for the sale of the property were John Green Richardson of Bath and his wife Mary, the daughter of Dr. Lincoln of Brunswick; Frederick L. and his wife Mary (Bartlett) Richardson; George L. Richardson of Topsham, and Henry Richardson of Boston. John transacted the business. He held public offices in Bath and was mayor in 1878-79.

Lucinda,[2] no dates found

Dorcas,[2] no dates found

Joseph,[2] b. 1803; d. 1804

Joseph W.,[2] (evidently named for the brother who died), b. 1804; m. Hannah P. Scannon

Jane,[2] b. in Saco, 1809; m. Robert Read

VI. The William King Family

WILLIAM, b. Feb. 9, 1768, at Scarborough; d. in Bath, Jan. 17, 1852. He m. Ann N. Frazier of Boston (b. 1782; d. in Portland, July 4, 1857) in 1800; and their children were:

Mary Elizabeth,[2] b. Sept. 28, 1817; d. unm. 1847

Cyrus William,[2] b. Dec. 25, 1819; m. Sarah Oakman Jameson, b. Aug. 28, 1823, dau. of Capt. James and Sarah (Randall) Jameson, on Oct. 19, 1853; d. April 16, 1881, in Brunswick. Sarah died July 31, 1895, also in Brunswick. Their children were:

William,[3] b. in Portland, July 18, 1856; graduated from Bowdoin, 1881; became a physician; d. Feb. 15, 1910, in Augusta.

Ann Nesbeth Frazier,[3] b. Jan. 31, 1860; m. (after 1884) Victor Minor, head floorwalker in a large Paris department store; d. 1908 in Paris (France).*

---

*In 1808, according to Henry W. Owen in his history of Bath *(op. cit.)*, John Richardson, the father of William, weathered the Embargo. His ship *Sally*, 342 t., with lumber for London, England, was sent to sea with two masters, Capt. James Rowe of Bath and Capt. Mackey of Scotland. They ran out of the river without clearance papers. William Richardson was supercargo on this voyage, which was the foundation of a fortune.

*Information obtained from James G. King, of Cambridge, Mass.

VII. The Benjamin Jones Porter Family

ELIZABETH (Betsy), the youngest daughter of Richard and Mary (Black) King, b. Jan. 7, 1770, m. Dr. Benjamin Jones Porter, who was b. in Beverly, Mass. He was educated at Byfield Academy and received his medical education with his uncle, Dr. Jones, who was a surgeon in the Continental Army in 1779. It is said that Dr. Porter served as a surgeon's assistant in Lafayette's regiment. He practiced in Scarborough and Stroudwater (now Westbrook and Portland). About 1792 or 1793, he went into business with William King in Topsham.

Before Maine's separation from Massachusetts, Porter served on the Governor's Council and as Senator from the District of Maine. He was treasurer of Bowdoin College (from which he received an honorary degree in 1809) from 1806 to 1815 when he got into financial difficulty, having lost $80,000 in the flood that caused so much damage to Topsham. He moved to Camden in 1829 and left his beautiful home and two vessels to William King to square his debts with him, ending their partnership.

Not much is said of Betsy, except that although she refused to attend affairs at the King house, she kindly took care of Mary Elizabeth when Ann King was sick.

Betsy and Dr. Porter are said to have had six children, but records of only four have been found in the King notes:

Rufus K.,[2] no dates
Charles R.,[2] no dates
Benjamin J.,[2] b. 1804 at Topsham; m. Arathusa, dau. of Phineas Bowers; d. Sept. 12, 1871, age 68. He was postmaster at Camden, 1853-61. They had seventeen children.
Mary,[2] no dates

VIII. The Cyrus King Family[*]

CYRUS, b. Sept. 6, 1772, youngest brother of Governor King, m. Hannah Storer, Oct. 1797; d. suddenly, April 25, 1817. He was, according to William H. Smith, "a fiery Federalist, defeated Richard Cutts, of Biddeford, brother-in-law of President James Madison, for Congress in 1812, and was re-elected in 1814...."[*]

The children of Cyrus and Hannah were:

Mary Caroline,[2] b. Jan. 27, 1799; m. Rev. Benjamin Hale,[8] April 9, 1823; d.

---

[*]Information provided from *Maine ... Recorder, op. cit.* (Vol. I, No. 2) pp. 33-34 in the article "The King Family of Maine," by Wm. H. Smith; and Vol. I, No. 4, pp. 209-11, in the article "Hon. Cyrus King and Some of His Family Connections," by the same author.

Jan. 22, 1867. Rev. Hale, b. Nov. 23, 1797, son of Thomas,[7] graduated at Bowdoin College in 1818, and after teaching a year at Saco Academy entered Andover Theological Seminary and was licensed to preach in Jan. 1822. He became a tutor in geometry and natural philosophy at Bowdoin, and from 1823 to 1827 was principal of the Lyceum at Gardiner, Me. He was a professor of chemistry at Dartmouth; became an Episcopalian, and took orders in that church; was at one time president of Hobart College in Geneva, N.Y. He d. at Newburyport, July 15, 1863.

The children of Mary Caroline and Dr. Hale were:

Caroline Olive,[3] b. Aug. 16, 1826; d. Feb. 9, 1837

Benjamin,[3] b. Oct. 31, 1827; m. Lucy Balch, Oct. 29, 1855. He became mayor of Newburyport, and they had two children.

Mary King,[3] b. April 3, 1830; d. Dec. 28, 1838

Sarah Elizabeth,[3] b. July 3, 1832; m. Rev. Malcolm Douglass of the Protestant Episcopal Church. They had seven children.

Thomas,[3] b. July 11, 1834; m. Lucy Frederic, dau. of Jotham and Elizabeth R. (Seavey) Green, Feb. 24, 1870. They had children.

Cyrus King,[3] b. Mar. 17, 1838; m. Alice Little Hale, May 7, 1866; d. June 5, 1874, and left four sons.

Josiah Little,[3] b. April 1, 1841; m. Annie Skinner, dau. of Jacob Willard and Mary B. (Dean) Pierce, April 24, 1873. He graduated from Hobart College in 1860, studied medicine at Harvard Medical School and in Europe, and practiced his profession in Brookline, Mass. The children of Josiah and Annie were:

Josiah,[4] b. Mar. 6, 1874; d. April 16, 1874

Mary Dean,[4] b. Mar. 15, 1876

Richard King,[4] b. March 17, 1880

A daughter,[4] b. Dec. 1, 1881

Ann Frazier,[2] b. Dec. 20, 1800, m. Edmund Theodore Bridge,[7] Sept. 1822. He was b. Dec. 6, 1799, and was the son of James,[6] and a descendant of John,[1] who came to America in Hooker's Company and settled in Cambridge, Mass., in 1632, and became a man of prominence. Edmund's grandfather Edmund[5] moved from Lexington, Mass., to Pownalboro in 1760. Hon. James, Edmund's father, was a distinguished man of rare ability. Edmund d. at Jersey City, N.J., Feb. 17, 1854. He and Ann had seven children, but no male issue lived to adult years. A brother of Edmund, James Bridge, m. Sarah Bowdoin, dau. of Hon. Ruel Williams of Augusta; and another brother, Horatio, was a classmate and warm personal friend of Nathaniel Hawthorne.

Olive Storer,[2] b. Dec. 15, 1802; m. Lauriston Ward, Nov. 1, 1838; and had two children. One d. unm.; the other, Caroline, m. Rev. Samuel J. Evans, and had one daughter.

William Rufus,[2] b. Nov. 16, 1804, graduated at Bowdoin College, 1823; d. 1836, unm. He was a lawyer of rare ability.

Elizabeth Porter,[2] b. Feb. 17, 1807; d. unm. Oct. 3, 1869

GENERAL WILLIAM KING 171

Hannah Storer,[2] b. Feb. 7, 1815; m. R. H. Haywood of Buffalo, N.Y.; d. Nov. 6, 1880. No children.

As of 1884, the children of Cyrus and Hannah King were all dead and none of their descendants were living in Maine.

Notes

I

1. *Maine Historical . . . Recorder,* "The Mansion and Tomb of Richard King of Scarborough," II, 2, 127.

II

1. *Memorial Volume on Popham Celebration.* August 29, 1862.
2. Eve Merriam, *Growing Up Female in America: Ten Lives.* New York: Dell Publishing Co., 1971, p. 31.
3. Anderson, J. F. "Recollections of Gen. King, First Governor of Maine," *Maine Historical . . . Recorder.* I, 3 (1884), p. 105 (quoting John H. Sheppard).
4. Ibid., p. 95 (quoting Deane Dudley).

III

1. Henry Owen, *History of Bath,* p. 139.
2. Parker Reed, *History of Bath,* p. 332.
3. Ibid., pp. 331-32.
4. Ibid., p. 334.
5. Ibid., p. 333.
6. Ibid., pp. 335-36.

IV

1. Anderson, op. cit., pp. 95, 96 (quoting Deane Dudley).
2. Ibid., p. 105-06 (quoting John H. Sheppard).

VI

1. William D. Williamson, *History of Maine*, II, 632.
2. From the collection of King papers belonging to Jane Stevens of Bath, who has kindly given us permission to reproduce this letter.
3. *Sprague's Journal of Maine History* XII (1924) 4, 243.
4. Fairburn, *Merchant Sail*, II, 840-41.
5. Owen, *op. cit.*, p. 150.
6. J. Henry Cartland, *Twenty Years at Pemaquid*, 5th verse of "A Song of 1812." Boothbay Harbor: L. A. Moore Printer, 1914, pp. 202-03.
7. Owen, *op. cit.*, p. 151.
8. *Ibid.*, pp. 155-56.
9. King Letters, Box 12 (1815).
10. *Ibid.*

VII

1. From the collection of King papers belonging to Jane Stevens of Bath, who has kindly given us permission to reproduce this letter.

VIII

1. Louis C. Hatch, *Maine, A History*, I, 149.
2. *Ibid.*

IX

1. King Letters, Box 16 (1818).
2. *Ibid.*
3. *Ibid.*, Box 17 (1819).
4. *Ibid.*

X

1. Hatch, *op. cit.*, p. 170.
2. Owen, *op. cit.*, pp. 166-67.
3. Hatch, *op. cit.*, p. 175.
4. Williamson, *op. cit.*, II, 679.

XI

1. Hatch, *op. cit.*, p. 175.
2. King Letters, Box 19 (1821).
3. *Ibid.*, Box 21.

4. *Ibid.*, Box 22.
5. Hatch, *op. cit.*, p. 184.
6. *Ibid.*
7. Reed, *op. cit.*, p. 86.
8. *Ibid.*, p. 88.

XII

1. Owen, *op. cit.*, p. 165.
2. *Ibid.*, p. 174.
3. *Maine . . . Recorder,* II, 1, p. 50.
4. Owen, *op. cit.*, p. 176.
5. From the collection of Jane Stevens of Bath, who has kindly given us permission to reproduce the letter.
6. David Saville Muzzey, pp. 223-224.
7. Hatch, *op. cit.*, pp. 193-94.
8. Hale-King Papers.

XIII

1. Hatch, *op. cit.*, p. 219.
2. *Ibid.*
3. Reed, *op. cit.*, pp. 334-35.
4. From the collection of Jane Stevens of Bath, who has kindly given us permission to reproduce the letter.
5. Quoted by J. F. Anderson, *Maine . . . Recorder,* I, 3, p. 98.

XIV

1. Hale-King Papers.
2. *Ibid.*
3. A controversy over the actual location of William King's grave arose many years later through numerous articles written by Allie King Gammon, a grandnephew of King, who believed that the Governor was buried in the old cemetery at Scarborough where Richard and Mary King, William's parents, and other relatives were buried. The D.A.R. had placed a plaque there in honor of Richard and his contribution to the early history of the town, and Gammon believed it was in commemoration of William. The articles Gammon had distributed were so widely publicized that a *Bath Daily Times* reporter, Robert Huse, dug into the files of the *Northern Tribune* and found the account of the funeral. Gammon was contacted and was convinced of his error after reading the report.
4. *Maine . . . Recorder,* II, 1, p. 50.

Bibliography

Andrews, Charles M., *A Short History of England.* Boston, Mass.: Allyn and Bacon, 1912.
Baker, Wm. A., *A Maritime History of Bath, Maine & The Kennebec Region,* Vol. I & II, produced under the direction of the Maritime History Committee, Marine Research Committee of Bath, Maine. Portland, Me.: Anthoenson Press, 1973, printer.
Banks, Ronald F., *Maine Becomes a State.* Middletown, Conn.: Wesleyan University Press, 1970.
Hatch, Louis Clinton, *Maine, A History* (Centennial Edition, 3 vols.). New York: The American Historical Society, 1919.
Fairburn, William Armstrong, *Merchant Sail,* 2 Vols. Center Lovell, Maine: Fairburn Marine Educational Foundation, 1945-1958.
Lemont, Levi P., *1400 Historical Dates of the Town and City of Bath and Town of Georgetown from 1604 to 1874.* Bath: Published by the author, 1874.
_____, *Memorial Volume of Popham Celebration, Aug. 29, 1862.*
Maine Historical and Genealogical Recorder (9 volumes), Vols. I & II. Portland, Maine: S. M. Watson, 1884-85.
Maine Historical Society *Newsletter* (12 volumes), Vol. II, 3.
Maine Writers' Research Club, *Maine Past and Present.* Boston, Mass.: D. C. Heath & Co., 1929.
Moulton, Augustus F., *Grandfather Tales of Scarborough.* Lewiston, Maine: Lewiston Journal Press, 1925.
_____, *Maine Historical Sketches.* Katahdin Pub. Co., 1926.
_____, *Portland by the Sea.* Katahdin Pub. Co., 1926.
Muzzey, David Saville, *An American History.* Boston, Mass.: Ginn and Company, 1920 Edition.

Owen, Henry W., Jr., *The Edward Clarence Plummer History of Bath*. Bath: The Times Company, 1936.

Pollard, Ralph J., *History of the Grand Lodge of Maine, A.F. & A.M., 1820 to 1925*. Portland, Maine: Tucker Printing Co.

Reed, Parker McCobb, *History of Bath and Environs, 1607-1894*. Portland, Maine: Lakeside Press, 1894.

Robinson, Ruel, *History of Camden and Rockport, Me*. Camden: Camden Publishing Co., 1907.

Spencer, Wilbur D., *Maine Immortals*. Augusta, Maine: Northeastern Press, 1932.

Torrey, W., *Bath Notorial Records*. Vol. 6. Bath: Bath Marine Museum Collection.

Varney, George J., *A Brief History of Maine*. Portland, Maine: McLellan, Mosier & Co., 1888.

Wheeler, George A. and Henry W., *History of Brunswick, Topsham, and Harpswell*. Boston, Mass.: Alfred Mudge & Son, 1878.

Williamson, William D., *The History of the State of Maine* (2 vols., Facsimile of the 1932 Edition). Freeport, Maine: The Cumberland Press, Inc., 1966.

Winthur, Oscar O. and William H. Cartwright, *The Story of Our Heritage*. Boston, Mass.: Ginn & Company, 1962.

Workers of the Federal Writer's Project, *Maine, A Guide Down East*. Boston, Mass.: Houghton Mifflin Co., 1937.

Index

Act of Separation, 103
Adams, John (U.S. president), 32
Adams, John Quincy (U.S. president), 109, 114, 115, 127
Alexander, 25, 38-39, 146-147
Allen, Horatio G., 45
Allen, William, 92
Ames, Benjamin, 60, 102, 110
Ames, Nathan, 60, 116, 117
Amiens, Peace of, 25
Anderson, James, 26
Anti-separationists, 86, 87
Appleton, Jesse, 80, 92
Ayer, Samuel, 87

Bab, Robert, 130
Ballard, Calvin (captain), 38-39, 146-147
Baptists, 83, 89
Barney, Joshua, 50
Batelle (King's agent), 84-85
Bath, Maine, 16
Bath Bank, 27
Berkley (British admiral), 34
Berry, Rufus, 83, 110
Betterment Act (1808), 28-29
Bingham Purchase, 28, 106. *See also* Kingfield
Blockade, 33, 49-54, 58, 79
Blyth (captain), 52
Bosworth, John, 33, 125
Bosworth, Robert (captain), 24, 26, 149-150, 158
Bowdoin College, 79-80, 83, 91-92, 134

Boxer, 52
Boyd, Joseph C., 102
Boynton, Abel, 45
Bridge, Ann Frazier, 126, 135-138, 170
British East Indies, 13
British Licenses, 50
Brooks, John (general), 55
Brunswick Cotton Factory, 81
Bulfinch, Charles, 122

Camden, Maine, 43, 45, 54
Captains, duties of, 11, 41-42
Carleton, Moses, 33, 36, 90
Chandler (general), 87, 111
Chandler, John, 102, 109
Chesapeake, 34
Clapp, Ebenezer (major), 59
Clarke, John, 16
Coastal Trade Laws, 86, 89, 90
Colby College, 84n
Collector of Customs, 36
Columbus (as name of state), 90-91
Congregationalists, 20, 83, 92
Congress. *See* United States Congress
Cone, Sam, 112
Constitution, Maine, 91, 92
Constitutional Convention, 1787 (United States), 5, 32
Constitutional Convention, 1816 (Maine), 88
Constitutional Convention, 1819 (Maine), 90
Continental Congress, 5
Cony, Daniel, 90-91, 103

Cook, Orchard, 36
Cotton industry, 24, 81, 106
Cotton trade, 24, 26
Crawford, William H., 89, 109, 114, 115, 127
Creek Indians, 108
Crooker, Isiah, 16
Cumberland Turnpike, 28
Cushing, Sylvanus, 10
Cushing, Tilson, 21
Customs, Collector of, 36
Customs laws: between states, 86; as obstacles to separation, 89; revised, 90

Dana, Judah, 92
Davenport, Benjamin (captain), 44
Davis, Jonathan, 16
Davis, Samuel, 21, 119
Dearborn, Henry (general), 45, 48, 53, 61, 82, 104-105
Democrat-Republicans, 32-33
Democrats, 128-129. *See also* Republican party; Democrat-Republicans
District of Maine. *See* Maine, District of
Dolbier, James, 134
Dudley, Deane, 12
Dudley, Nathaniel, 131
Dunlap, Robert P., 128, 129, 141
Dyett, Mark, 25

Eastern Argus, 87, 89, 90, 128
Education, public, 91
Embargo Act of 1807, 35-37, 43
Emerson, William, 52
England. *See* Great Britain
Enterprise, 52
Eustis, William, 45

Fair American, 33-34, 149
Falmouth Gazette, 86
Federalist party, 43, 80, 105, 114, 115; at Bowdoin College, 83; constitutional convention supported by, 32-33; in Massachusetts, 58, 88, 89, 92; political appointments for, 101
Ferdinand, 26-27, 149-150
Fields, Elizabeth, 125, 126
Florida, 108-109, 111
Foote, Erastus, 45, 102
Fort St. Georges, 57
Fort Sullivan, 48
France, 11, 13, 25-26, 33, 40. *See also* Non-intercourse law (1809); Embargo Act of 1807
Frazier, Ann, 18, 19. *See also* King, Ann N. Frazier
Frazier, John, 18, 33
Frazier, Mary Caroline, 126
French Assembly, 11

Gallatin, Albert, 115
General Court of the Commonwealth of Massachusetts, 22, 35, 43, 58, 83, 87-88, 89
Ghent, Treaty of, 61
Governor of Maine, King elected, 100-101
Great Britain, 25, 43; harassment of American shipping by, 34-35; trade laws of, 39; trade with, 11, 13, 23, 33, 39-40, 50. *See also* Non-intercourse Law (1809); Embargo Act of 1807; orders in Council
Great Seal of the State of Maine, 103
Green, Ballard, 110
Green, Peter H., 18, 33, 52, 110, 124
Greenleaf, Simon, 102
Greenwood, Andrew, 59

Hale, Rev. Benjamin, 169-170
Hamilton, Alexander, 11, 32
Harding, Nehemiah (captain), 24
Hartford Convention, 53
Hill, John Langdon, 54
Hill, Mark Langdon, 58, 93, 98, 109, 116, 117

Hinckley, Hester, 126
Holmes, John, 87, 102, 109, 115, 128
Houghton, Levi, 118
Hyde, Jonathan, 119
Hyde, Zina, 45, 54, 60

Ice, 125
Illicit trade, 38, 116
Impressment, 34, 39, 44
Industrial Revolution (in England), 24, 25

Jackson, Andrew (U.S. president), 108-109, 123, 127-128, 129
Jay's Treaty (1794), 13
Jefferson, Thomas (U.S. president), 33, 35, 91, 104
Jenks, Rev. William, 22, 45, 54-55
Junto (of separationists), 87-89

Kennebec, 83
Kennebec ice, 125
King, Ann N. Frazier (1782-1857), 12, 18-19, 22, 28, 33, 36, 94-98, 101, 103, 104, 110-111, 114, 119-122, 134, 136, 141, 142, 168
King, Cyrus (1772-1817), 3, 8, 32, 81, 169; family of, 169
King, Cyrus William (1819-1881), 98, 121-123, 133, 134, 142, 168
King, Edward, 116, 163
King, Isabella Bragdon (1764-1770), 2, 3, 167
King, James Gore (b. 1791), 82, 115, 161
King, Mary (nee Black), 2, 5, 81
King, Mary Caroline (1799-1867), 81, 169
King, Mary Elizabeth (1817-1847), 83, 94, 98, 121, 126, 134, 168
King, Paulina (b. 1759), 2, 165; family of, 165
King, Richard (William's father), 1-2, 3
King, Richard Jr. (1762-1830), 3, 166; family of, 166
King, Rufus (1775-1827), 2-5, 32, 36, 89, 93, 115, 159; family of, 159
King, William (1768-1852), 3, 4, 18, 19, 84, 134, 135-141, 168; appearance of, 12, 29-30, 120; business interests of, 7, 9-10, 16, 27, 28, 30, 31, 33, 79, 125, 106; character of, 5, 9, 20, 30, 44, 49, 120, 132-133; civic and religious activities of, 20-21, 83-84, 98, 119; as commissioner of public buildings, 121; as customs collector, 117, 124, 127; decline of, 79-80, 82, 125, 127-134; at General Court of Massachusetts, 12, 22, 35, 43, 83, 88; as governor (1820-1821), 100-101, 105; gubernatorial nomination of (1835), 128; lieutenant governor candidacy of, 82; liquor prohibition favored by, 21-22, 113; at Maine Constitutional Convention, 90; as major-general, 43-48, 53, 55-62; political views of, 33, 91-92, 101-102, 106, 107; real estate of, 28, 30, 130-131, 133. *See also* Kingfield; Stonehouse Farm; King mansion; shipping business of, 35-37, 38-40, 116-117, 125, 132; as Spanish Claims Commissioner, 109-110; vice presidential nomination of, 115
King, William Rufus (1804-1836), 81, 170
Kingfield, 28, 29, 110, 121, 131, 132, 134. *See also* Bingham Purchase
King George's War, 1
King mansion, 19-20, 120, 134, 142
King monument, 142-143
King statue (U.S. Capitol), 143
Knapp, Ruth, 131
Know Nothing Party, 22
Knox, Mrs. Henry, 80-81; property of, 31, 80
Knox, Harry (Henry Jr.), 80-81

Lane, John, 25, 152-153
Lane (captain), 26-27, 149-150
Lapish, Robert, 10
Lee, Silas, 25
Leland, Dorcas King (b. 1766), 3, 167-168; family of, 168
Leland, Joseph, 81, 168
Lemont, Thomas, 21
Leopard, 34
Lieutenant Governor, offices of, 103
Lime business, 110
Linches Law, 125
Lincoln and Kennebec Bank of Wiscasset, 27, 33
Literacy, 91
Louisburg, 2
Louisiana Purchase, 108
Louisiana Territory, 26

McClellan, James, 45
McCobb, Denny (general), 44, 54, 55, 58-60
Macon Act, 39-40
Madison, James (U.S. president), 37, 39, 53
Madison's Nightcaps, 58
Maine, defense of (War of 1812), 43, 44-45, 48, 53-60
Maine, District of, 11, 43; militia quota from, 44
Maine, name of, 90-91
Maine, Province of, 11
Maine Agricultural Society, 106
Maine Constitution, 91, 92
Maine Constitutional Convention (1819), 90
Maine Governor, King elected, 100-101
Maine Literary and Theological Institution for Baptists, 83, 89
Maine Statehood Bill, 92
Maine State Legislature, 101, 106, 107, 114, 142
Maine State Seal, 103

Margaretta, 52-53
Marine Insurance Company of Boston, 27, 33, 79, 125
Marston, Joshua, 49
Masons, 98, 128, 140-141
Massachusetts; cooperation with British 51. *See also* Hartford Convention; neglected Maine defense, 43, 45, 46, 53, 55, 58, 62, 86
Massachusetts, General Court of. *See* General Court of the Commonwealth of Massachusetts
Massachusetts Legislature, 83
Mellen, Prentiss, 102
Methodists, 89
Militia (Maine), 44-45, 48, 53-54
Miller, James (general), 61
Million Acre Farm, 28, 29, 131, 134
Missouri Compromise, 93
Monroe, James (U.S. president), 61, 108-109, 116
Moody, William, 102
Moses, Oliver, 119
Moses, William V., 119
Moses Boats, 10
Mud Clippers, 58

Nancy, 25, 152-153
Napoleon Bonaparte, 13, 25-26, 33, 40
National Republicans, 128
Navy. *See* United States Navy
Neutral nations (War of 1812), 13-14, 51, 79
New Orleans trade, 24
Non-importation Act, 50
Non-intercourse Law (1809), 37-39, 43
North Church (Bath), 21
Nymph, 14, 50-51, 153

Old South Church (Bath), 22
Oliver, James (captain), 39, 156
Orders in Council, 33, 36, 37, 41, 44
Oregon Territory, 109

Orne, Henry, 110
Orr, Benjamin, 80
Osiris, 14-15, 153
Otis, Harrison Gray, 28

Page, Edward, 19
Page, John O., 38-39
Parris, Albion, 87, 110, 112
Parties, political. *See* Federalist party, Democrat-Republicans, Republican party
Patronage, political, 102, 106
Patten, George F., 118-119, 141
Patten, John, 118-119, 141
Patten Library Association, 141
Payson, David, 90
Peace of Amiens, 25
Pepperell, William, 2
Petitions (for separation), 86
Pettis, John (captain), 44
Pinckney Treaty, 13, 24
Piper, Amos, 52
Political patronage, 102, 106
Popham Fort, 59, 60
Porter, Aaron, 165
Porter, Benjamin Jones, 5, 7, 8, 9, 18, 24, 33, 79-80, 109, 169
Porter, Elizabeth King (b. 1770), 3, 5, 81, 169
Porter, Mary, 80, 165
Porter, Paulina King (b. 1759), 165
Porter, Richard K., 40, 156, 165
Porter, Ruth Knapp, 131
Porter, Seward, 83
Porter, William K., 59
Porter and King — Merchants, 7-10, 13, 26, 39, 169
Portland, Maine, 104
Portland Gazette, 87
Preble, William Pitt, 87, 88, 90, 100, 102
Privateers, 1, 13, 14, 38, 50, 51
Public education, 91
Public lands, 107

Purington, Ezekiel (captain), 84-85, 156
Putnam, Perley, 48
Putnam, Samuel, 46

Ratford, Jenkin, 34
Raymond (captain), 14, 153
Recruitment (War of 1812), 45-48
Redington, Asa, 134, 141
Redman, Tristam (captain), 14-15, 153
Reed, Andrew (colonel), 44, 54, 58, 59
Republican party, 43, 80, 91, 92, 102, 105, 114-116
Richardson, Harriet Leland, 36, 168
Richardson, John, 36
Richardson, William, 36, 133, 134, 168, 168n
Rideout, Johnson, 119
Ring, John, 38-39
Robinson, Thomas, 134

Saco, Academy, 165
St. Georges, Fort, 57
Savage, John, 33
Seminole Indians, 108-109
Separation (Maine from Massachusetts), 86-90, 92-93
Separation, Act of, 88, 103
Separation, Articles of, 92
Separation Convention (1816), 88
Separationists, 88
Sewall, Dummer, 16, 20, 21
Sewall, Samuel, 54
Sewall, William D., 119
Shaving Mills, 46, 46n
Shaw, Joshua, 21
Shipbuilding: techniques, 17; decline of, 121
Ship captains: duties of, 11, 41-42
Shipping business: description of, 23-24; in 1820s, 118-119
Shipyards, 9, 17
Slavery, 92-93
Smith, Ezra, 24

Smith, Perham, 102
Smuggling, 35, 36, 48, 51, 54
Sons of Liberty, 3
South Church (Bath), 21-22
Southgate, Eliza, 9, 18, 164
Southgate, Mary King (1757-1824), 2, 164; family of, 164
Southgate, Dr. Robert, 4, 164
South Society, 22
Spain, 13, 50, 108-109; claims against by American merchants, 109, 110
Spanish Claims Commission, 116
Spanish Treaty, 109, 111
Sprague, Peleg, 128
Squatters, 28
Stanley, Solomon, 29
Statehood (Maine), 93, 100-101
Statehood Bill, 92
State House, 122, 128
Steam engines, 82-83
Stern, William, 48
Stonehouse Farm, 30, 31, 83, 110
Strong, Caleb, 45, 53, 58, 62
Stuart, Gilbert, 12
Sullivan, Fort, 48
Sullivan, John (general), 4
Swanton, John B., 117

Tallman, Peleg, 12, 16, 28, 33, 36, 51, 55
Tariff of Abominations, 124, 127
Tariffs, 124, 132
Timber cutting, 109
Toleration Act (1811), 22
Toll bridge (Topsham-Brunswick), 11
Tom Thumb, 82-83
Torrey, William (captain), 44
Tory, 3
Trade, illicit, 38, 116
Trade embargo law. *See* Embargo Act of 1807
Trade laws between states, 86, 89, 90
Treaty of Ghent (1814), 61
Treaty of 1783, 61

Typhys, 84-85, 156

Ulmer, George (colonel), 48
Ulmer, Philip (major), 48
United States, 39-40, 156
United States banks, 127, 129
United States Congress, 11, 89, 114; passes Embargo Act, 35; passes Nonintercourse Act, 37; passes Macon Act, 39
United States Navy: British harassment of, 34, 39, 44; merchant vessels protected by, 25

Van Buren, Martin (U.S. president), 115
Volunteers (War of 1812), 45
Vose, Robert C., 90

Ware, Ashur, 102
Ware of 1812, 44-61; Fort St. Georges burned in, 57, Maine towns captured in, 54; Sheepscot expedition, 55, 60
Waterville College, 84n
Wells's School for Moral Discipline, 122-123, 133
West Indies trade, 10, 11, 26, 41, 106, 108, 118, 124, 125; British interruption of, 25; after Jay's Treaty, 13
Weston, Nathan, 102
Whigs, 128
Whiting, Samuel, 87, 88
Whitman, Ezekiel, 102
Williams, Johnson, 119
Williamson, William D., 102, 106, 110
Wilson, John (captain), 44
Wingate, Joshua Jr. (general), 96, 104-105, 111, 112
Wingate, Joseph, 95, 96, 114, 116
Winter of 1816-1817, 81
Wiscasset Bank, 27, 33
Wood, Abiel, 33, 36

Zetetic Club, 129-130